From the Ashes to the Stars: 50 Events that Propelled Civilization

by
Matthew King

* * * * *

Published by Matthew King

From the Ashes to the Stars: 50 Events that Propelled
Civilization
Copyright© 2024 by Matthew King

Table of Contents

INTRODUCTION

In the vast tapestry of human history, there are threads that shimmer brightly, weaving the story of our collective journey from the ashes of ancient times to the dazzling stars of the modern era. "From the Ashes to the Stars: 50 Events that Propelled Civilization" embarks on an enlightening exploration of pivotal moments that have left an indelible mark on the course of human development.

Each event unfolds as a chapter in the grand narrative of our shared existence, revealing not only the challenges faced but the triumphs achieved. From the annals of antiquity to the cutting-edge frontiers of contemporary society, these 50 events serve as celestial beacons guiding our understanding of the profound changes that have shaped the world.

This journey traverses epochs and cultures, unearthing the roots of our civilizations and tracing the interconnectedness of societies across time. The book delves into the profound impact of wars, revolutions, scientific breakthroughs, cultural movements, and the relentless pursuit of knowledge. It seeks to unravel the complex tapestry of human achievement, drawing connections between seemingly disparate events that collectively propelled us forward.

As we embark on this odyssey, let us reflect on the transformative power of the human spirit. From the embers of destruction to the brilliance of innovation, each chapter tells a story of resilience, adaptation, and the relentless pursuit of progress. "From the Ashes to the Stars" invites readers to ponder the legacy of these 50 events, exploring how they have sculpted the world we inhabit today and continue to shape the limitless possibilities of our future.

Chapter 1: The Agricultural Revolution

In the crucible of necessity and innovation, humanity took a transformative step forward with the advent of the Agricultural Revolution. This pivotal chapter in our history unfolded over millennia, forever altering the course of human civilization as we transitioned from nomadic hunter-gatherer lifestyles to settled agricultural communities.

20,000 BCE: Earliest Signs of Human Influence on Wild Grains in Israel

The journey towards agricultural mastery begins as early as 20,000 BCE in the region that is now Israel. Archaeological evidence reveals the first glimpses of humans exerting control over wild grain, marking the initial steps towards plant domestication.

11,000 BCE: Cultivation and Trait Selection of Rye in Syria and Diverse Domestications in Greece

Around 11,000 BCE, a significant milestone is reached in Syria with planned cultivation and trait selection of rye. Concurrently, in Greece, evidence surfaces of the domestication of various crops, including lentils, vetch, pistachios, and almonds, showcasing a growing mastery over diverse plant species.

9,500 BCE: Eight Key Crops Domesticated in the Levant

By 9,500 BCE, the Levant, encompassing regions such as Syria, Lebanon, Palestine, Israel, Jordan, Cyprus, and Turkey, witnesses the domestication of eight key crops. Emmer wheat, einkorn wheat, barley, peas, lentils, bitter vetch, chickpeas, and flax become staples, laying the foundation for settled agricultural communities.

9,100 BCE: Oldest Known Agricultural Settlement at Klimonas, Cyprus

Klimonas, Cyprus, became the site of the oldest known agricultural settlement around 9,100 BCE. This marks a crucial moment where humans transition from nomadic lifestyles to establishing permanent communities based on the cultivation of crops.

9,000 BCE: Domestication of Sheep and the Establishment of Farming Along the Nile River

By this time, around 9,000 BCE, the domestication of sheep takes place in various locations in central and southwest Asia. Simultaneously, farming is fully established along the Nile River in Egypt, marking the inception of one of the world's great agricultural civilizations.

8,000 BCE: Agricultural Expansion in Mesopotamia, China, and the Domestication of Various Animals

Farming becomes fully established along the Tigris and Euphrates rivers in Mesopotamia (Iraq), and rice and millet are domesticated in China. This era witnesses the domestication of goats in Iran, pigs in the Near East, China, and Germany, and the cultivation of maize and squash in Mexico.

7,000 BCE: Agricultural Flourishing in Mesopotamia and the Indus Valley, and the Domestication of Cattle

Mesopotamia witnesses the flourishing of agriculture around 7,000 BCE, while evidence of the first agricultural practices surfaces in the Indus Valley (Pakistan, India). Additionally, cattle are domesticated in North Africa, India, and Mesopotamia, further transforming human societies.

6,000 BCE: Agriculture Reaches the Iberian Peninsula, and the Domestication of Chickens and Llamas

Agriculture reaches the Iberian Peninsula (Spain, Portugal) around 6,000 BCE. Simultaneously, chickens are domesticated in India and Southeast Asia, while llamas are domesticated in Peru, showcasing the global spread of agricultural practices.

5,500 BCE: Advanced Farming Practices in Sumeria

Farmers in Sumeria (Iraq) make significant strides around 5,500 BCE, developing large-scale intensive cultivation of land, mono-cropping, organized irrigation, and a specialized agricultural labor force. These advancements lay the groundwork for more complex and sophisticated societies.

5,000 BCE: Domestication of Rice and Sorghum in Africa's Sahel Region

Around 5,000 BCE, the Sahel region in Africa experiences the domestication of rice and sorghum. This marks a crucial development in African agriculture, contributing to the diversity of crops cultivated on the continent.

4,000 BCE: Domestication of the Horse in Ukraine and Kazakhstan

The nomadic lifestyle was forever altered around 4,000 BCE with the domestication of the horse in Ukraine and Kazakhstan. This marks a crucial moment in transportation and agricultural practices.

3,700 BCE: Oldest Known Field Systems in Ireland

In Ireland, around 3,700 BCE, the landscape transforms with the establishment of the oldest known field systems, including stone walls. This showcases the global diversity in agricultural practices and the unique adaptations to local environments.

3,000 BCE: Introduction of the Ox-drawn Ard Plow in Egypt

Around 3,000 BCE in Egypt, the earliest known use of the ox-drawn ard plow revolutionized farming practices. This innovation enhances the efficiency of cultivation, marking a technological leap in agricultural history.

As we journey through these chronological milestones, it becomes evident that the Agricultural Revolution was a cumulative effort spanning diverse regions, cultures, and crops. Each development represents a pivotal moment in human history, shaping the foundations of civilization through the mastery of the land and the domestication of plants and animals.

Chapter 2: The First Cities Emerge in Mesopotamia

In the cradle of civilization, along the fertile banks of the Tigris and Euphrates rivers, a profound transformation unfolded. Mesopotamia, the land between the rivers, bore witness to the birth of the world's first cities, marking a pivotal moment in the annals of human history.

This chapter delves into the emergence of these early urban centers, exploring their origins, growth, and the enduring impact they had on the course of human civilization.

5400 BCE: The Legendary Beginning at Eridu

According to legend, around 5400 BCE, the Sumerians laid the foundations for their first settlement in Mesopotamia at Eridu. This legendary origin story represents the nascent stages of organized human habitation, as communities sought to establish a foothold in the fertile landscapes provided by the region's mighty rivers.

4500 BCE: Uruk Rises as the First City

Around 4500 BCE, the Sumerian settlement of Uruk emerged as the first true city in Mesopotamia. Uruk's rise marked a significant shift from scattered villages to a concentrated urban center, characterized by complex social structures, monumental architecture, and the convergence of diverse communities.

2900 BCE: Uruk Claims the Title of the World's Largest City

By 2900 BCE, Uruk reached unprecedented heights, claiming the title of the world's largest city. The cityscape of Uruk sprawled with ziggurats, temples, and crowded markets, reflecting the burgeoning complexity of urban life. The scale of Uruk's influence reverberated across the ancient world, setting new standards for what a city could achieve.

2075 BCE: Lagash Takes Center Stage

Around 2075 BCE, the Sumerian city of Lagash surpassed its predecessors, becoming the largest city in the world. This transition showcased the dynamic nature of

Mesopotamian urban development, as Lagash rose to prominence with its own unique character, contributing to the rich tapestry of ancient city-states.

2030 BCE: Ur Ascends to Supremacy

The city of Ur, around 2030 BCE, claimed the mantle of the world's largest city, succeeding Lagash in this prestigious title. As a testament to the continued growth and dynamism of Mesopotamian society, Ur stood as a beacon of cultural and economic power, leaving an indelible mark on the evolving narrative of human civilization.

In exploring the rise of these cities, we unravel the intricate threads that wove the fabric of ancient Mesopotamian society. The emergence of cities in this region not only marked a shift in architectural scale but also laid the groundwork for monumental advancements in governance, trade, and cultural expression.

As we journey through the corridors of time, the story of the first cities in Mesopotamia unfolds, revealing the foundations upon which subsequent civilizations would build and innovate.

Chapter 3: The First Wheeled Vehicles

In the grand saga of human innovation, the development of wheeled vehicles stands as a monumental leap forward. This chapter delves into the fascinating history of the first wheeled vehicles, tracing their origins in the ancient landscapes of Mesopotamia, Eastern Europe, and the Caucasus.

From humble beginnings to transformative impacts on trade and transportation, the story of the wheel's introduction unfolds, marking a revolutionary chapter in the annals of human technological advancement.

3500 BCE: Mesopotamia and the Birth of the Wheeled Cart

Around 3500 BCE, the flat plains of Mesopotamia witnessed a groundbreaking innovation—the birth of the wheeled cart. Initially, these early carts served as indispensable tools for transporting goods, easing the burden on human and animal labor. The simple wheel and axle design set the stage for a revolution in transportation that would echo through the corridors of time.

3300 BCE: Wheeling into Eastern Europe

As the wheels of progress turned, the knowledge of wheeled vehicles traversed across regions. Around 3300 BCE, wheeled vehicles made their appearance in Eastern Europe, becoming a driving force in the transformation of local economies and societies. The wheels, once set in motion, rolled their way into the fabric of daily life.

3000 BCE: The Caucasus Embraces the Wheel

In the rugged terrains of the Caucasus, around 3000 BCE, the innovation of wheeled vehicles found a new foothold. The adaptation of this technology in the mountainous landscapes reflected the versatility and adaptability of the wheel, proving its utility across diverse geographical and cultural settings.

2500 BCE: The Evolution of Wheeled Vehicles

By 2500 BCE, wheeled vehicles underwent significant evolution. From basic carts, more sophisticated chariots emerged, transforming not only transportation but also warfare. The speed and maneuverability of chariots made them formidable tools in the hands of military strategists, reshaping the dynamics of ancient conflicts.

2000 BCE: Wheels and the Silk Roads

The integration of wheeled vehicles into trade routes, including the famed Silk Roads, became a defining feature of interconnected ancient civilizations. The wheels facilitated the movement of goods, ideas, and cultures across vast distances, fostering economic prosperity and cultural exchange on a global scale.

Legacy of the Wheel

The advent of wheeled vehicles ushered in a new era of human mobility and connectivity. Beyond the practical aspects of transportation, the wheel became a symbol of progress, innovation, and the human drive to overcome the challenges of terrain and distance. Its legacy endures in modern society, where wheels continue to be instrumental in shaping our world.

As we explore the emergence of wheeled vehicles in Mesopotamia, Eastern Europe, and the Caucasus, we uncover not only the technological achievements of ancient societies but also the profound impact that a simple yet ingenious invention can have on the course of human history. The wheel, once set into motion, rolled its way into the heart of civilization, leaving an indelible mark on the journey of humanity.

Chapter 4: The First Writing Systems Appear

In the crucible of ancient civilizations, a monumental leap in human communication unfolded with the emergence of the first writing systems. This chapter explores the birth of written language in three distinct cradles of civilization: Mesopotamia, where cuneiform left its indelible mark; Egypt, where hieroglyphics adorned monumental structures; and the Indus Valley, where the enigmatic Indus Script hinted at a sophisticated ancient script.

These early writing systems not only served practical functions but also became powerful conduits for preserving knowledge, recording history, and shaping the cultural identities of their respective societies.

3200 BCE: Mesopotamia and the Birth of Cuneiform

Around 3200 BCE, in the fertile plains of Mesopotamia, the Sumerians pioneered the first known writing system—

cuneiform. Initially etched on clay tablets with wedge-shaped marks, cuneiform evolved from accounting symbols to a comprehensive script capable of recording narratives, laws, and literature. Mesopotamian society was forever transformed as the written word became a vessel for the transmission of knowledge and culture.

3100 BCE: Egypt and the Majestic Hieroglyphics

In the ancient sands of Egypt, around 3100 BCE, hieroglyphics emerged as a script inscribed on monumental structures and religious texts. With its intricate pictorial symbols, hieroglyphics adorned the walls of temples and tombs, chronicling the stories of pharaohs, religious rites, and the daily life of the ancient Egyptians. The enduring elegance of hieroglyphics reflected the cultural richness and sophistication of Egypt.

2600 BCE: The Enigma of the Indus Script

In the mysterious realm of the Indus Valley, around 2600 BCE, the Indus Script made its appearance. Despite its elegance and consistency, the script remains an enigma, as scholars grapple with decoding its meaning and purpose. Stamped onto seals and artifacts, the Indus Script leaves behind a silent testimony to the advanced civilization that thrived along the banks of the Indus River.

2000 BCE: Cuneiform Evolves in Mesopotamia

As Mesopotamian societies expanded and evolved, so too did the cuneiform script. By 2000 BCE, cuneiform had diversified into various styles, with distinct scripts for Sumerian, Akkadian, and other languages.

This evolution mirrored the changing political and cultural landscapes of Mesopotamia, where writing became an essential tool for administration, diplomacy, and intellectual pursuits.

1300 BCE: Hieroglyphics and the Rosetta Stone

In Egypt, around 1300 BCE, the Rosetta Stone became a pivotal key to unlocking the mysteries of hieroglyphics. The stone, inscribed with the same text in three scripts—hieroglyphics, demotic, and Greek—provided a crucial bridge for deciphering the ancient Egyptian script. The Rosetta Stone heralded a new era in understanding the rich history encoded in hieroglyphics.

Legacy of Ancient Scripts

The legacy of cuneiform, hieroglyphics, and the Indus Script extends far beyond the eras of their creation. These early writing systems not only facilitated communication but also became vessels for religious texts, legal codes, literature, and historical records. They laid the groundwork for the development of subsequent writing systems and the preservation of human knowledge.

As we unravel the stories encoded in cuneiform, hieroglyphics, and the Indus Script, we gain insights into the intellectual achievements, cultural identities, and aspirations of ancient societies.

These scripts, etched onto clay tablets, temple walls, and seals, serve as windows into the minds of our forebears, revealing the transformative power of the written word in shaping the course of human civilization.

Chapter 5: The Ancient Egyptians

In the heart of the Egyptian desert, a colossal testament to human ingenuity and engineering prowess rises from the sandy expanse—the Great Pyramid of Giza. Built during the reign of Pharaoh Khufu, this monumental structure stands as an enduring symbol of ancient Egyptian civilization.

This chapter delves into the remarkable story of the construction of the Great Pyramid, exploring the motivations, techniques, and cultural significance behind the creation of one of the Seven Wonders of the Ancient World.

2580–2560 BCE: The Vision of Pharaoh Khufu

Around 2580–2560 BCE, during the Fourth Dynasty of the Old Kingdom, Pharaoh Khufu envisioned a grand burial structure that would not only immortalize his legacy but also serve as a gateway to the afterlife. The Great Pyramid was conceived as a testament to the divine authority of the pharaoh and the eternal nature of Egyptian civilization.

Design and Planning: The Architectural Marvel

The design and planning of the Great Pyramid reveal a profound understanding of geometry, astronomy, and engineering. The structure's base covers an area of over 13 acres, and its sides align precisely with the cardinal points of the compass. The precision in design suggests a sophisticated level of knowledge and planning, with the pyramid serving as a monumental symbol of cosmic alignment.

Workforce: Labor from Across the Nile

The construction of the Great Pyramid required an immense workforce, estimated to be in the tens of thousands. Laborers were drawn from across the Nile region, including skilled craftsmen, engineers, and an army of unskilled workers. The workforce was organized into hierarchical groups, with overseers, laborers, and skilled artisans collaborating to bring Khufu's vision to life.

Construction Techniques: Precision in Stone

The construction techniques employed in building the Great Pyramid showcase the ancient Egyptians' mastery of quarrying, transporting, and shaping massive limestone and granite blocks.

The precision with which the stones were cut and fitted together is a testament to the advanced engineering skills of the builders. Theories on the use of ramps, levers, and sledges abound, yet the exact methods remain a subject of scholarly debate.

Religious Significance: A Pathway to the Afterlife

Beyond its monumental size and architectural precision, the Great Pyramid held profound religious significance. Aligned with the belief in an afterlife, the pyramid was designed to secure Khufu's journey to the realm of the gods. The interior passages and chambers contained intricate religious texts and symbols, emphasizing the connection between the earthly and divine realms.

Legacy: The Enduring Wonder

The completion of the Great Pyramid marked not only a triumph of engineering but also a lasting legacy that has captivated the world for millennia. As the tallest man-made structure for over 3,800 years, the pyramid has inspired awe, speculation, and admiration.

Its enduring presence reflects the ancient Egyptians' commitment to monumental architecture as a medium for immortalizing their pharaohs and asserting the grandeur of their civilization.

As we explore the story of the Great Pyramid of Giza, we unravel the mysteries and marvels that surround its construction. From the vision of Pharaoh Khufu to the labor of thousands, from precise engineering to religious symbolism, the Great Pyramid stands as an enduring testament to the heights of human achievement in the ancient world.

Chapter 6: The Origin and Development of Modern Alphabets

The evolution of written communication has been a journey of creativity and ingenuity, with modern alphabets standing as a testament to the human quest for efficient and versatile means of expressing language. This chapter explores the origin and development of modern alphabets, tracing their evolution from ancient scripts to the diverse writing systems used today.

From the Phoenician alphabet to the Roman script and beyond, the story of modern alphabets reflects the dynamic interplay of cultures, civilizations, and the enduring human need for effective written communication.

The Phoenician Alphabet

The roots of modern alphabets trace back to the ancient Phoenicians, who, around 1200 BCE, devised a revolutionary script based on a system of 22 consonantal symbols. The Phoenician alphabet served as a concise and adaptable writing system, laying the foundation for the diverse alphabets that would follow.

800–300 BCE: The Spread of Alphabets in the Mediterranean

The Phoenician alphabet found its way to Greece, where it underwent modifications to incorporate vowels. This innovation marked a crucial development, transforming the script into a more versatile tool for representing spoken language. The Greek alphabet, emerging around 800 BCE, became a key influence on later European scripts.

500 BCE: The Roman Script Emerges

The Roman script, the precursor to many modern Western alphabets, evolved from the Etruscan alphabet around 500 BCE. As the Roman Empire expanded, so did the influence of its script, paving the way for the development of alphabets used in numerous European languages.

400–600 CE: The Spread of Alphabets to Northern Europe

The Latin script, derived from the Roman alphabet, spread northward as the Roman Empire expanded. As various Germanic and Celtic tribes adopted the Latin script, they infused it with their linguistic nuances, giving rise to distinct alphabets for languages such as Old English and Old High German.

800–1500 CE: The Development of Vernacular Scripts

During the Middle Ages, the use of written language expanded beyond Latin, giving rise to vernacular scripts adapted for regional languages. Scripts such as the Gothic script in Northern Europe and the Italic script in Italy reflected the linguistic diversity of the evolving European landscape.

15th Century CE: The Printing Press Revolutionizes Alphabets

The invention of the printing press in the 15th century by Johannes Gutenberg marked a transformative moment in the history of alphabets. As movable type facilitated mass production of books, standardized scripts such as the Carolingian minuscule became widespread, fostering increased literacy and the dissemination of knowledge.

18th–19th Century CE: The Rise of National Scripts

As nations emerged in Europe, the standardization of written languages led to the development of national scripts. Linguistic reforms in countries like France and Germany resulted in the creation of alphabets tailored to the unique phonetic characteristics of each language, contributing to linguistic identity and cultural expression.

20th Century CE to Present: Globalization and Digital Alphabets

The 20th century witnessed the globalization of alphabets as writing systems adapted to the demands of international communication. The advent of digital technology further transformed the way alphabets are used, with computer fonts, keyboards, and the internet influencing the way people read and write across the globe.

Alphabets in the Digital Age

In the 21st century, alphabets continue to evolve in response to the demands of a digitally interconnected world. The story of modern alphabets, from their ancient origins to their contemporary forms, reflects the enduring human endeavor to communicate effectively across languages and cultures. As technology advances, the journey of alphabets persists, adapting to new mediums and ensuring the continued evolution of written language.

Chapter 7: The Code of Hammurabi

In the heart of ancient Mesopotamia, around 1754 BCE, the Babylonian King Hammurabi issued a groundbreaking document that would resonate through the ages—the Code of Hammurabi.

This chapter delves into the historical and cultural context of this ancient legal code, exploring its significance as one of the earliest known systems of laws and its enduring impact on the development of legal thought and governance.

1792–1750 BCE: The Reign of Hammurabi

King Hammurabi ascended to the throne of Babylon during a period of territorial expansion and consolidation of power. His reign marked a pivotal moment in the history of Mesopotamia, and it was during this time that the Code of Hammurabi was promulgated, likely between 1792 and 1750 BCE.

Purpose and Context: Establishing Justice in Babylon

The Code of Hammurabi was conceived to address the complexities of governance and justice in a growing and diverse society. Hammurabi sought to establish a comprehensive set of laws that would govern various aspects of Babylonian life, from commerce and family matters to criminal conduct and religious practices.

Content and Structure: The Laws of Hammurabi

Comprising 282 laws inscribed on a monumental stele, the Code of Hammurabi is a detailed legal document that covers a wide array of subjects. The laws are organized thematically, addressing issues such as property rights, contracts, marriage and family matters, labor relations, and criminal offenses. The severity of punishments often varied based on the social status of the individuals involved.

Legal Principles: Retribution and Social Order

The Code of Hammurabi is characterized by a system of retributive justice, where punishments are designed to fit the nature of the crime. The principle of "an eye for an eye" reflects a belief in proportionate justice. The code also codifies certain aspects of social hierarchy and provides specific guidelines for resolving disputes within the Babylonian society.

Influence on Later Legal Systems

The Code of Hammurabi had a profound influence on the development of legal thought and systems in the ancient world. While not the first legal code, it stands out for its comprehensive nature and the insight it provides into the values and norms of Babylonian society. Elements of Hammurabi's legal principles can be traced in later legal codes, including those of the Hittites, Assyrians, and even aspects of Roman law.

The Stele of Hammurabi: An Architectural Testament

The Code of Hammurabi was inscribed on a large diorite stele, standing over seven feet tall. The stele, now displayed in the Louvre Museum in Paris, features a relief sculpture of Hammurabi receiving the laws from the god Shamash. This visual representation underscores the divine authority attributed to the laws and emphasizes the king's role as a just ruler.

Legacy: Hammurabi's Enduring Impact

Hammurabi's legal code represents a foundational moment in the history of jurisprudence. Its legacy endures not only as one of the earliest known legal systems but also as a testament to the intricate interplay between law, governance, and societal values in the ancient world.

The Code of Hammurabi provides modern scholars with valuable insights into the legal and social structures of ancient Mesopotamia, showcasing the roots of legal thought that have shaped civilizations throughout history.

Chapter 8: The Bronze Age Ends and the Iron Age Begins

In the crucible of technological advancement, a transformative moment emerged as ancient societies began to unlock the secrets of iron metallurgy. This chapter explores the pivotal transition from the Bronze Age to the Iron Age, a period marked by the widespread adoption of iron tools and weapons. As knowledge of ironworking spread, it ushered in an era of profound changes in weaponry, agriculture, and infrastructure, reshaping the course of human history.

The Bronze Age: A Metallurgical Epoch

The Bronze Age, characterized by the widespread use of bronze—an alloy of copper and tin—spanned millennia, shaping the rise of early civilizations. Bronze tools, weapons, and artifacts defined this era, contributing to the cultural and economic prosperity of societies from Mesopotamia to the Mediterranean.

1200 BCE: The Collapse of Bronze

Around 1200 BCE, the Bronze Age faced a series of disruptions, including invasions, migrations, and political upheavals. Traditional trade routes collapsed, and established power structures weakened. These destabilizing factors, along with the scarcity of tin, a crucial component of bronze, contributed to the decline of the Bronze Age civilizations.

Iron: Abundant and Accessible

Unlike the scarce and region-specific resources required for bronze, iron was abundant and widely distributed. The shift to iron metallurgy marked a turning point, as societies discovered the benefits of utilizing this more readily available resource. Iron ores, such as hematite and magnetite, were abundant, paving the way for a widespread adoption of iron tools and weapons.

Technological Advancements: Ironworking Secrets Unveiled

Ironworking required higher temperatures than bronze, necessitating new techniques and technologies. The development of hotter furnaces and more efficient bellows allowed for the extraction of iron from its ores.

The transformative process of carburization, in which iron was heated with carbon-rich substances, produced steel, a material that surpassed bronze in strength and durability.

Iron Tools: A Revolution in Agriculture and Industry

The widespread adoption of iron tools revolutionized agriculture and industry. Iron plows, axes, and hoes enabled more efficient cultivation and land clearance, leading to increased agricultural productivity. Iron also played a crucial role in the development of machinery, facilitating advancements in mining, construction, and manufacturing.

Iron Weapons: The Changing Face of Warfare

The availability of iron transformed the landscape of warfare. Iron weapons, including swords, spears, and arrowheads, offered advantages in strength and sharpness over their bronze counterparts. The Iron Age witnessed the rise of powerful military empires that harnessed the capabilities of iron weaponry to expand and assert dominance.

Iron Age Civilizations: New Centers of Power

The widespread use of iron contributed to the emergence of new centers of power and cultural innovation. Iron Age civilizations, such as the Neo-Assyrian Empire, the Kingdom of Israel, and later the Roman Empire, flourished and left a lasting impact on the course of history. Iron became a symbol of progress and dominance in the ancient world.

Legacy: Iron's Enduring Impact

The transition from the Bronze Age to the Iron Age marked a fundamental shift in the trajectory of human progress. Iron's versatility and abundance transformed not only technology and warfare but also societal structures and economic systems.

The legacy of the Iron Age endures in the tools, artifacts, and structures that have withstood the test of time, reflecting the resilience and adaptability of human societies across millennia.

Chapter 9: The Rise of Ancient Greek Civilization

The ancient Greek civilization stands as a beacon of human achievement, influencing philosophy, politics, arts, and sciences across the Mediterranean and beyond.

This chapter explores the multifaceted rise of Ancient Greece, from its humble beginnings to the zenith of its cultural and political prowess. Through the lens of city-states, philosophy, arts, and the Olympics, we unravel the intricate tapestry of Greek civilization that has left an enduring legacy on Western thought and culture.

Minoans and Mycenaeans: Foundations of Greek Civilization

The roots of Ancient Greek civilization trace back to the Minoans and Mycenaeans, early cultures that thrived in the

Aegean region during the Bronze Age. The Minoan civilization on Crete, with its advanced art and maritime prowess, laid the groundwork for the Mycenaeans, who incorporated both warlike and cultural elements into their society.

800–500 BCE: The Age of the City-States (Polis)

The emergence of city-states, or polis, marked a defining feature of Ancient Greek civilization. Independent and self-governing, city-states such as Athens, Sparta, and Corinth became the crucibles of Greek culture, fostering democratic ideals, civic engagement, and distinctive regional identities.

Athens: The Birthplace of Democracy

Athens, the cultural and intellectual epicenter of Ancient Greece, birthed the concept of democracy. The reforms of leaders like Cleisthenes and Pericles transformed Athens into a direct democracy, where citizens participated in decision-making processes. This experiment in governance laid the groundwork for modern democratic principles.

Sparta: A Military State

In stark contrast, Sparta emerged as a military powerhouse. Governed by a dual monarchy and an oligarchic system, Sparta focused on martial discipline and prowess. The Spartans' militaristic ethos, exemplified by the renowned Spartan phalanx, shaped the city-state's identity and played a crucial role in its historical legacy.

Philosophy: The Birth of Rational Inquiry

Ancient Greece witnessed a remarkable era of intellectual exploration, with philosophers like Socrates, Plato, and Aristotle laying the foundations of Western philosophy. Socratic dialogue, the Platonic Academy, and Aristotelian logic became cornerstones of critical thinking, paving the way for profound inquiries into ethics, metaphysics, and the nature of existence.

The Arts: Drama, Sculpture, and Architecture

The Ancient Greeks excelled in the arts, creating enduring masterpieces that continue to captivate the world. Greek drama, exemplified by the works of playwrights like Aeschylus, Sophocles, and Euripides, explored profound themes. Sculpture, as seen in the statues of athletes and gods, expressed idealized human forms, while architecture, epitomized by the Parthenon, showcased harmony, balance, and the pursuit of perfection.

The Olympic Games: A Celebration of Athleticism and Unity

The Olympic Games, held in Olympia, were a manifestation of Greek ideals and values. Dating back to 776 BCE, the Games celebrated athletic prowess, fostering a sense of unity among Greek city-states during periods of peace. The sacred truce ensured safe passage for athletes and spectators, highlighting the interconnectedness of Greek culture.

323–146 BCE: The Hellenistic Period

Following the conquests of Alexander the Great, the Hellenistic period witnessed the spread of Greek culture across the vast territories of the Macedonian Empire. The fusion of Greek, Egyptian, Persian, and other influences gave rise to a rich tapestry of cultural achievements, contributing to the Hellenistic legacy.

Legacy: Greek Civilization's Enduring Impact

The legacy of Ancient Greek civilization endures in the foundational principles of democracy, philosophy, arts, and sciences that continue to shape Western thought. From the halls of academia to the corridors of governance, the echoes of Ancient Greece resonate, reminding us of a civilization that reached unprecedented heights in human achievement and laid the groundwork for the intellectual and cultural traditions of the Western world.

Chapter 10: The Rise and Fall of Ancient Roman Civilization

The rise and fall of Ancient Rome constitute one of the most compelling narratives in human history. From its humble beginnings as a city-state on the Italian Peninsula to the heights of imperial power, Rome left an indelible mark on Western civilization.

This chapter explores the multifaceted journey of Ancient Rome, delving into its republican foundations, imperial expansions, cultural achievements, and the eventual challenges and decline that led to the fall of this once-mighty civilization.

509–27 BCE: The Roman Republic Emerges

The story of Ancient Rome begins with the establishment of the Roman Republic around 509 BCE, following the overthrow of the Roman monarchy. The principles of a representative government, the Senate, and the separation of powers laid the groundwork for Rome's republican institutions, where citizens played a central role in decision-making.

Expansion and Conquest: The Punic Wars and Imperial Growth

The Roman Republic embarked on a trajectory of territorial expansion, engaging in the Punic Wars with Carthage and gaining control over vast territories in the Mediterranean. The conquests of Gaul, Greece, and parts of Asia Minor expanded Roman influence, creating a sprawling empire.

27 BCE–180 CE: The Pax Romana

The transition from the Roman Republic to the Roman Empire marked a transformative era known as the Pax Romana, lasting from 27 BCE to 180 CE. Under the leadership of Augustus and subsequent emperors, Rome experienced a period of relative stability, economic prosperity, and cultural flourishing.

Roman Governance: The Imperial System

The governance of the Roman Empire evolved into a system characterized by a centralized autocracy. The emperors wielded significant power, and while the Senate retained some authority, the imperial system marked a departure from the republican ideals of the early Roman Republic.

Roman Law and Engineering: Pillars of Civilization

The Romans' contributions to law and engineering remain enduring aspects of their civilization. The development of Roman law, exemplified by the Twelve Tables, laid the foundation for legal principles that would influence Western legal systems. Roman engineering feats, such as aqueducts, roads, and monumental structures like the Colosseum, showcased their mastery of construction and infrastructure.

Cultural Achievements: Literature, Philosophy, and the Arts

Ancient Rome fostered a rich cultural milieu that produced influential literature, philosophy, and artistic achievements. Virgil's epic poem, the Aeneid, exemplified Roman literary prowess, while philosophers like Seneca and Cicero explored ethical and political ideas. Roman art and architecture, including realistic portraiture and grand structures like the Pantheon, reflected the aesthetic sophistication of the civilization.

Crisis and Decline: Economic Strain, Political Instability, and Invasions

Despite its zenith, Ancient Rome faced internal and external challenges that contributed to its decline. Economic strain, political corruption, military overextension, and invasions by barbarian tribes weakened the empire. The Crisis of the Third Century saw a period of political instability and fragmentation, leading to the eventual fall of the Western Roman Empire.

476 CE: The Fall of the Western Roman Empire

The year 476 CE is often cited as the symbolic date of the fall of the Western Roman Empire. The last Roman emperor, Romulus Augustulus, was deposed by the Germanic chieftain Odoacer. The fall of Rome marked the end of an epoch and the beginning of the Middle Ages in Europe.

Legacy: The Enduring Influence of Rome

The legacy of Ancient Rome endures in modern Western civilization. Roman legal principles, governance structures, language (Latin), and cultural achievements have left an indelible mark.

The concept of the Roman Empire, spanning centuries and vast territories, continues to resonate as a symbol of power, governance, and cultural achievement in the annals of human history.

Chapter 11: The Life of the Buddha

In the 6th century BCE, in the region of present-day Nepal, a profound spiritual journey unfolded that would give birth to one of the world's major religions – Buddhism.

This chapter delves into the life of Siddhartha Gautama, who later became known as the Buddha, and explores the foundational teachings and principles that shaped the emergence of Buddhism as a transformative force in the quest for enlightenment and liberation from suffering.

Siddhartha Gautama: The Early Years

Born into the Sakya clan in Lumbini, Nepal, around 563 BCE, Siddhartha Gautama grew up in the lap of luxury. Shielded from the harsh realities of life, Siddhartha's early years were marked by privilege and indulgence. However, his father, King Suddhodana, sought to protect him from the suffering inherent in the world.

The Four Sights: Encounters with Suffering

Despite his protected upbringing, Siddhartha's curiosity led him to venture beyond the palace walls. During these excursions, he encountered the Four Sights—a sick person, an old person, a corpse, and a wandering ascetic. These sights exposed Siddhartha to the unavoidable realities of human suffering and impermanence, prompting him to seek answers to life's fundamental questions.

The Great Renunciation: The Ascetic Path

Driven by a deep yearning for truth, Siddhartha made the momentous decision to renounce his princely life. He left behind his family, wealth, and palace comforts to embark on a spiritual quest. Adopting the life of an ascetic, he engaged in rigorous practices of self-mortification under various teachers, determined to unravel the mysteries of existence.

Enlightenment Under the Bodhi Tree

After years of ascetic practices brought him no closer to enlightenment, Siddhartha abandoned extreme austerities and sought a middle way. Seated beneath the Bodhi Tree in Bodh Gaya, India, he entered deep meditation, vowing not to rise until he attained enlightenment. On the night of the full moon in May, he reached a state of profound understanding and became the Buddha, the "Awakened One."

The First Sermon: The Turning of the Wheel of Dharma

Following his enlightenment, the Buddha traveled to Sarnath, where he delivered his first sermon to five ascetics. Known as the Deer Park Sermon or Dhammacakkappavattana Sutta, the discourse outlined the Four Noble Truths—the foundation of Buddhist philosophy. The Buddha expounded on the nature of suffering, its origin, cessation, and the path leading to liberation from suffering.

The Four Noble Truths: The Core Teachings

Dukkha (Suffering): Life is characterized by suffering, unsatisfactoriness, and impermanence.

Samudaya (Origin of Suffering): The cause of suffering is craving and attachment.

Nirodha (Cessation of Suffering): Suffering can be extinguished by eliminating craving and attachment.

Magga (Path to the Cessation of Suffering): The Eightfold Path outlines the ethical and mental practices leading to enlightenment.

The Eightfold Path: The Way to Liberation

The Eightfold Path, often depicted as a wheel, delineates the ethical and mental practices essential for overcoming suffering and achieving enlightenment. The path encompasses right understanding, intention, speech, action, livelihood, effort, mindfulness, and concentration.

The Sangha and the Spread of Buddhism

The Buddha, having established a community of followers known as the Sangha, spent the remaining years of his life teaching and guiding disciples. The Sangha, consisting of monks and nuns, played a crucial role in preserving and disseminating the Buddha's teachings. Buddhism gradually spread across India and beyond, adapting to diverse cultures and evolving into various schools and traditions.

The Parinirvana: The Buddha's Passing

Around 483 BCE, at the age of 80, the Buddha attained Parinirvana, the final passing away. His last teachings emphasized the impermanence of all things and the importance of individual effort in the pursuit of liberation. The Buddha's death marked the end of his earthly journey, but his teachings continued to resonate and guide countless followers in the centuries that followed.

Legacy: Buddhism's Global Impact

The life of the Buddha and the birth of Buddhism left an enduring legacy that transcended time and geography. Buddhism spread throughout Asia and beyond, influencing art, philosophy, and culture. Its teachings on compassion, mindfulness, and the nature of existence continue to inspire millions of people seeking a path to inner peace and enlightenment.

Chapter 12: The Life of Confucius

In the midst of ancient China, during the tumultuous period of the Eastern Zhou dynasty, a profound sage emerged whose teachings would shape the moral and ethical fabric of Chinese society for centuries to come.

This chapter delves into the life of Confucius, known as Kong Fuzi or Master Kong, and explores the foundational principles of Confucianism—a philosophical and ethical system that has profoundly influenced Chinese culture, governance, and morality.

Confucius: Early Life and Education

Born in 551 BCE in the state of Lu (modern-day Shandong province, China), Confucius' early life was marked by modesty and intellectual curiosity. Orphaned at an early age, he sought knowledge and immersed himself in the study of traditional Chinese classics and rituals. His commitment to learning and moral rectitude set the stage for the development of Confucian philosophy.

Career as a Teacher and Public Official

Confucius pursued a career as a teacher, attracting disciples who were eager to learn from his wisdom. Despite his deep insights into governance and morality, Confucius faced challenges in securing a prominent position in government. He served in various minor roles, but his vision for ethical leadership clashed with the prevailing political climate of the time.

The Analects: Compilation of Confucian Teachings

The Analects, a collection of sayings and ideas attributed to Confucius, became the cornerstone of Confucian thought. Compiled by his disciples after his death, these teachings encapsulated Confucius' views on morality, virtue, family, governance, and the pursuit of a harmonious society. The Analects laid the groundwork for Confucianism as a moral and ethical guide.

Ren (Humaneness) and Li (Rituals): Core Concepts

Central to Confucianism are the concepts of ren and li. Ren, often translated as "humaneness" or "benevolence," underscores the importance of compassion, empathy, and ethical conduct in human interactions. Li, representing rituals and proper conduct, emphasizes the significance of traditional ceremonies, manners, and social harmony as essential elements of a virtuous society.

Filial Piety and the Five Relationships

Confucianism places significant importance on familial relationships, particularly the concept of filial piety (xiao). Filial piety involves respecting and honoring one's parents and ancestors, considering it a fundamental virtue.

Confucius also emphasized the Five Relationships—ruler and subject, father and son, husband and wife, elder and younger siblings, and friend and friend—as integral to social harmony.

Rectification of Names and Ethical Governance

Confucius believed in the rectification of names (zhengming) as a means to ensure ethical governance. This concept emphasized the importance of using language accurately and ethically to reflect the true nature of relationships and responsibilities. He advocated for leaders to be virtuous and to embody moral qualities that would inspire the populace to follow a path of righteousness.

Confucianism and Later Development

Following Confucius' death in 479 BCE, his disciples continued to propagate his teachings, and Confucianism gradually gained prominence in Chinese intellectual and cultural circles. Despite periods of suppression and revival, Confucianism persisted through the centuries and became deeply ingrained in Chinese thought, influencing governance, education, and societal values.

Neo-Confucianism: Revival and Synthesis

During the Song dynasty (960–1279 CE), Neo-Confucianism emerged as a revival and synthesis of Confucian thought with elements of Daoism and Buddhism. Scholars like Zhu Xi played a pivotal role in shaping Neo-Confucian philosophy, emphasizing metaphysical principles alongside ethical teachings. Neo-Confucianism became the dominant intellectual force in China for centuries.

Confucianism in East Asian Cultures

Confucianism spread beyond China and became a profound influence on East Asian cultures, including

Korea, Japan, and Vietnam. Confucian principles shaped societal norms, education systems, and governance structures in these regions, leaving an indelible mark on their cultural identity.

Contemporary Significance: Confucianism in the Modern World

Confucian values continue to resonate in the modern world, influencing ethical considerations, family dynamics, and societal norms. While Confucianism has adapted to changing times, its core emphasis on moral integrity, harmonious relationships, and the pursuit of a just and humane society endures, demonstrating the enduring impact of Confucius and the birth of Confucianism.

Chapter 13: Alexander the Great

In the annals of ancient history, few names echo with the resonance of Alexander the Great—a visionary military strategist and conqueror who, in a remarkably short span, forged one of the largest empires the world had ever seen.

This chapter delves into the life and conquests of Alexander, exploring the factors that propelled him to greatness and examining the vast empire he created, which stretched from Greece to Egypt, Persia, and beyond.

Alexander's Early Life and Education

Born in Pella, the capital of Macedon, in 356 BCE, Alexander was the son of King Philip II and Queen Olympias. Raised in the court of Macedon, he received a classical education under the renowned philosopher Aristotle. The teachings of Aristotle instilled in Alexander a love for literature, philosophy, and the arts, complementing his martial prowess.

Ascension to the Throne: The Macedonian Conquests

Following the assassination of King Philip II in 336 BCE, the 20-year-old Alexander ascended to the throne of Macedon. Determined to fulfill his father's dream of conquering Persia, Alexander swiftly consolidated his power in Greece and embarked on a series of military campaigns, known as the Macedonian Conquests, to secure his dominance over Greek city-states.

The Battle of Issus and Conquest of Persia

In 333 BCE, Alexander faced Persian King Darius III at the Battle of Issus. Despite being outnumbered, Alexander's strategic brilliance secured a decisive victory. This triumph opened the gates to Persia, and in 331 BCE, he decisively defeated Darius at the Battle of Gaugamela, effectively ending Persian resistance and securing Alexander's control over the Persian Empire.

The Conquest of Egypt and the Founding of Alexandria

After the fall of Persia, Alexander turned his attention to Egypt, where he was welcomed as a liberator. In 332 BCE, he founded the city of Alexandria, a cultural and commercial hub that would later become one of the greatest cities of the ancient world. The Oracle at Siwa declared him the son of Zeus-Ammon, reinforcing his divine status.

The Indian Campaign and the Battle of Hydaspes

Driven by an insatiable appetite for conquest, Alexander continued eastward into the Indian subcontinent. His army faced formidable challenges, including the Battle of Hydaspes against King Porus. Although victorious, Alexander's troops, exhausted and homesick, prompted him to curtail further eastward expansion, marking the farthest extent of his conquests.

Hellenistic Synthesis: The Fusion of Cultures

As Alexander's empire expanded, a cultural fusion known as the Hellenistic Synthesis took shape. Greek ideas, art, and language melded with the diverse cultures of conquered territories, creating a dynamic blend that enriched the arts, sciences, and philosophy. This cultural exchange laid the groundwork for the Hellenistic period that followed.

The Death of Alexander and the Division of the Empire

In 323 BCE, at the age of 32, Alexander succumbed to illness in Babylon. His untimely death left a power vacuum, leading to a protracted struggle among his generals, known as the Diadochi, for control over the empire. Ultimately, the empire was divided into several successor states, each led by a Diadoch, marking the beginning of the Hellenistic era.

Legacy: Alexander's Impact on History and Culture

Alexander's conquests left an indelible mark on the course of history and culture. The spread of Hellenistic influence fostered the rise of great cities, the flourishing of arts and sciences, and the dissemination of Greek philosophy. The concept of the "Alexander Romance" further immortalized his exploits, influencing literature, art, and the imagination of generations to come.

Alexandria: Legacy of a Great Conqueror

One of the most enduring legacies of Alexander's empire is the city of Alexandria. A center of learning, trade, and culture, Alexandria became a beacon of Hellenistic civilization. Its famed library, the Library of Alexandria, housed an immense collection of scrolls and served as a testament to the intellectual richness that emerged from the crossroads of cultures.

Alexander's Conquests in Perspective

While Alexander's empire did not endure in its unified form, his conquests reshaped the geopolitical landscape and initiated a new era of cultural interchange. The Hellenistic world that emerged from his endeavors laid the foundation for the subsequent rise of Rome and the enduring impact of Greek culture on the Western world. Alexander's legacy as a conqueror and cultural catalyst endures as a testament to the transformative power of visionary leadership and the pursuit of greatness.

Chapter 14: Unification of China

In the annals of ancient China, one name stands out as a pivotal figure in the unification of a fractured land and the initiation of monumental construction projects—the First Emperor, Qin Shi Huang.

This chapter explores the life and reign of Qin Shi Huang, detailing the unification of China and the commencement of the construction of the Great Wall, a testament to the emperor's vision, ambition, and the enduring legacy of his rule.

Rise to Power: The Qin Dynasty Emerges

Born as Ying Zheng in 259 BCE, Qin Shi Huang ascended to the throne of the Qin state at the age of 13. His reign marked the consolidation of power and the effective end of the Warring States period—a tumultuous era characterized by incessant warfare among regional states vying for supremacy.

Unification of China: The Qin Dynasty Conquests

Qin Shi Huang, determined to unify China under his rule, launched a series of military campaigns against rival states. Employing a combination of military strategy and political cunning, he systematically defeated his adversaries. In 221 BCE, Qin Shi Huang achieved his vision, proclaiming himself Qin Shi Huangdi—the First Emperor of the Qin Dynasty and the ruler of a unified China.

Standardization: Currency, Writing, and Measurement

In his quest for unity, Qin Shi Huang implemented radical reforms to standardize various aspects of Chinese society. He introduced a uniform system of currency, standardized the Chinese script, and established a common system of weights and measures. These measures were intended to promote administrative efficiency and cultural homogeneity across the newly unified empire.

Terracotta Army: Guardians of the Afterlife

One of the most extraordinary achievements of Qin Shi Huang's reign was the construction of the Terracotta Army. Located near his burial site, these life-sized clay soldiers, horses, and chariots were created to accompany the emperor in the afterlife. The Terracotta Army is a testament to Qin Shi Huang's belief in the continuation of imperial authority beyond death.

Construction of the Great Wall Begins

Recognizing the need for defensive structures to protect against nomadic invasions from the north, Qin Shi Huang initiated the construction of the Great Wall of China.

The project involved connecting and extending existing fortifications, creating a formidable barrier against potential invaders. While the wall underwent significant expansion and modification in subsequent dynasties, Qin Shi Huang's efforts laid the foundation for this iconic structure.

The Qin Legal Code: Authoritarian Governance

Qin Shi Huang implemented a comprehensive legal code aimed at centralizing authority and maintaining strict social control. The code was characterized by severe punishments for offenses, reflecting Qin Shi Huang's emphasis on maintaining order and obedience within the empire. This authoritarian approach to governance left a lasting impact on the legal and administrative systems of subsequent Chinese dynasties.

Death and Legacy: The Controversial First Emperor

In 210 BCE, Qin Shi Huang died at the age of 49 during a tour of his empire. His death led to a brief period of chaos and the eventual collapse of the Qin Dynasty. Despite controversies surrounding his rule, including the harsh measures employed to achieve unification, Qin Shi Huang left an enduring legacy as the first ruler to unite China and lay the groundwork for the imperial system that would persist for centuries.

Qin Shi Huang's Mausoleum: An Architectural Marvel

The tomb of Qin Shi Huang, believed to be located near Xi'an, has long been shrouded in mystery. According to historical accounts, the mausoleum is an immense complex that includes the Terracotta Army, palaces, and various treasures. The tomb remains unopened due to concerns over potential damage to the artifacts and the risk of mercury contamination.

The Enduring Impact of Qin Shi Huang

Qin Shi Huang's unification of China, his monumental construction projects, and his authoritarian governance style have left an indelible mark on Chinese history. While his rule was relatively short-lived, the impact of his policies and initiatives reverberated for centuries, shaping the foundations of imperial China.

The Great Wall, the Terracotta Army, and the standardization efforts remain tangible reminders of Qin Shi Huang's ambitious vision and the unification of a vast and diverse empire under a single ruler.

Chapter 15: The Birth of the Modern Calendar

The concept of timekeeping has been central to human civilization, reflecting our need to understand and organize the passage of days, months, and years. The birth of the modern calendar is a fascinating journey that involves the convergence of astronomical observations, cultural traditions, and the human quest for precision. This chapter explores the development of the modern calendar, delving into key historical milestones and the evolution of systems that have shaped our contemporary understanding of time.

Early Calendars: Celestial Observations and Cultural Significance

The earliest attempts at calendrical systems can be traced back to ancient civilizations that observed celestial events to mark the passage of time. From the lunar calendars of ancient Egypt and Mesopotamia to the solar calendars of ancient China, these early systems intertwined with cultural, religious, and agricultural practices.

The Roman Calendar: A Lunar Foundation

The Roman calendar, believed to be derived from the lunar calendar of the ancient Greeks, was initially based on a lunar cycle. However, with only 354 days in a lunar year, it required regular adjustments to align with the solar year. The introduction of intercalation, the addition of extra days or months, aimed to correct discrepancies but often led to confusion.

The Julian Calendar: Aligning with the Solar Year

In 45 BCE, Julius Caesar implemented a calendar reform known as the Julian Calendar. Collaborating with the Alexandrian astronomer Sosigenes, the Julian Calendar shifted towards a solar-based system with a 365-day year and an additional day every four years—what we now know as a leap year. This marked a significant improvement in synchronizing the calendar with the Earth's orbit around the sun.

The Gregorian Calendar: Fine-Tuning for Accuracy

Over time, it became evident that the Julian Calendar's leap year adjustment still introduced a slight discrepancy. In 1582, Pope Gregory XIII introduced the Gregorian Calendar, further refining the leap year rule to better align with the solar year. The Gregorian Calendar is the calendar most widely used today, with its adoption by Catholic countries and later acceptance across the world.

Adoption and Globalization of the Gregorian Calendar

The widespread adoption of the Gregorian Calendar unfolded gradually over centuries. Catholic countries in Europe embraced the new calendar in 1582, while Protestant countries and others followed suit in the subsequent centuries. The adoption process varied across regions, leading to a mix of Julian and Gregorian systems in use for some time.

Cultural and Religious Calendars: Diversity in Timekeeping

While the Gregorian Calendar serves as the international standard for civil purposes, various cultures and religions maintain their own calendars. The Islamic, Hebrew, Hindu, and Chinese calendars, among others, continue to play vital roles in religious observances, cultural traditions, and daily life for millions around the world.

Challenges and Reforms: Contemporary Calendar Adjustments

In the modern era, discussions about calendar reform have resurfaced, driven by the increasing precision of astronomical measurements. Proposals for calendar adjustments, such as the World Calendar or the Hanke-Henry Permanent Calendar, aim to simplify timekeeping and eliminate irregularities associated with leap years.

The Future of Calendars: Scientific Precision and Cultural Diversity

Advancements in astronomical knowledge and computational capabilities continue to refine our understanding of time. As we navigate the complexities of a globalized world, the question of whether to maintain cultural diversity in timekeeping or move towards a more standardized system remains an ongoing dialogue. The development of precision timekeeping, including atomic clocks and coordinated universal time (UTC), reflects our perpetual quest for accuracy in measuring the passage of time.

Time's Enduring Tapestry

The birth and evolution of the modern calendar weave a narrative that spans millennia, reflecting humanity's ceaseless endeavor to comprehend and organize time.

From ancient lunar cycles to the precision of contemporary atomic timekeeping, the calendar stands as a testament to our cultural, scientific, and philosophical pursuits. As we navigate the intricate tapestry of time, the calendar remains a dynamic expression of human ingenuity and our ongoing quest to capture the essence of temporal existence.

Chapter 16: The Life of Jesus and the Birth of Christianity

In the first century of the Common Era, in the region of Judea, a spiritual figure emerged whose teachings would profoundly impact the course of history and inspire the birth of a global faith—Christianity.

This chapter explores the life of Jesus of Nazareth and the pivotal moments that led to the foundation of Christianity, examining the teachings, events, and the enduring legacy of the man whose life and message would shape the beliefs of billions.

Jesus of Nazareth: Birth and Early Life

The exact birthdate of Jesus remains uncertain, but historical accounts place it around 4 to 6 BCE in Bethlehem. Raised in Nazareth by Mary and Joseph, Jesus grew up in relative obscurity. His early life is marked by few recorded events, with glimpses provided in the Gospels of the New Testament, particularly in the Gospel of Luke.

Baptism by John the Baptist: The Commencement of Ministry

Around the age of 30, Jesus began his public ministry with a significant event—the baptism by John the Baptist in the Jordan River. This symbolic act marked the initiation of Jesus' public mission, signifying a spiritual rebirth and the commencement of his teachings.

The Sermon on the Mount: Core Teachings

One of the most iconic moments in Jesus' ministry is the Sermon on the Mount, as recorded in the Gospel of Matthew. This sermon encapsulates essential elements of Jesus' teachings, including the Beatitudes, teachings on love and forgiveness, and the Lord's Prayer. The Sermon on the Mount remains a cornerstone of Christian ethics.

Miracles and Parables: Demonstrating Divine Power

Throughout his ministry, Jesus performed miracles, such as healing the sick, restoring sight to the blind, and even raising the dead. These acts were accompanied by parables—short, illustrative stories conveying moral and spiritual lessons. Miracles and parables served to illustrate Jesus' divine authority and illuminate the principles of the Kingdom of God.

The Twelve Apostles: Formation of a Core Group

As Jesus gained followers, he selected twelve disciples to be his closest companions and messengers—the Twelve Apostles. This inner circle witnessed Jesus' teachings, miracles, and engaged in personal instruction. The apostles would play a crucial role in the spread of Jesus' message after his death.

The Last Supper and the Betrayal

The Last Supper, a Passover meal, holds profound significance in Christian tradition. During this event, Jesus instituted the Eucharist, a symbolic ritual representing his body and blood. It was at the Last Supper that Jesus foretold his betrayal by one of his disciples, later identified as Judas Iscariot.

The Crucifixion: A Profound Sacrifice

The crucifixion of Jesus, an event central to Christian theology, took place in Jerusalem. Condemned by the Roman authorities and crucified alongside criminals, Jesus' death is viewed by Christians as a sacrificial atonement for humanity's sins. His last words, as recorded in the Gospels, include the famous cry, "Father, forgive them, for they know not what they do."

Resurrection and Ascension: Foundations of Christian Faith

Christianity's core tenet lies in the belief in the resurrection of Jesus on the third day after his crucifixion. According to Christian tradition, Jesus appeared to his disciples, providing proof of his victory over death. After forty days, Jesus ascended into heaven, a pivotal moment affirming his divine nature and marking the end of his earthly presence.

The Spread of Christianity: The Early Church

The disciples, empowered by the teachings and resurrection of Jesus, became the apostles who played a crucial role in spreading the Christian message. The Day of Pentecost, as described in the Book of Acts, marked the descent of the Holy Spirit upon the apostles, empowering them to communicate in various languages and embark on evangelizing missions.

The Apostle Paul: Architect of Christian Theology

Paul, formerly known as Saul, emerged as a significant figure in the early Christian movement. His conversion on the road to Damascus transformed him into a fervent advocate for Christianity. Paul's missionary journeys and epistles played a pivotal role in shaping Christian theology and spreading the message to diverse regions.

Persecutions and Martyrdom: A Faith Tested

In the early centuries, Christians faced sporadic persecution under Roman rule. Despite these challenges, the Christian community continued to grow, and the stories of martyrs, individuals who willingly faced persecution and death for their faith, became a testament to the resilience of Christian belief.

Formation of the New Testament: Canonization of Scriptures

Over time, a collection of writings emerged as authoritative for the Christian community. The process of canonization resulted in the formation of the New Testament, a compilation of Gospels, letters, and other writings that became the foundational scriptures of Christianity.

Council of Nicaea: Defining Christian Doctrine

In 325 CE, the Council of Nicaea convened to address theological controversies and define key aspects of Christian doctrine. The Nicene Creed, formulated during this council, articulated fundamental beliefs about the nature of Jesus and the Trinity, providing a doctrinal foundation for Christian orthodoxy.

The Enduring Legacy of Jesus and Christianity

The life of Jesus and the birth of Christianity have left an indelible mark on human history. Christianity, with its diverse denominations and interpretations, has become the world's largest religion. The life, teachings, death, and resurrection of Jesus continue to inspire billions of believers, shaping moral, ethical, and cultural landscapes across the globe. The story of Jesus stands as a testament to the enduring power of faith and the transformative impact of a single life on the course of human history.

Chapter 17: The Life of Muhammad and the Birth of Islam

In the early 7th century CE, in the deserts of Arabia, a spiritual revelation ignited a movement that would profoundly transform the religious and cultural landscape of the region and beyond. This chapter explores the life of Muhammad, the prophet of Islam, and the foundational moments that led to the birth of one of the world's major monotheistic religions—Islam.

Arabia in the 6th Century: Cultural and Religious Context

In the 6th century CE, the Arabian Peninsula was characterized by tribal societies and polytheistic beliefs. Mecca, a prominent trading center, housed the Kaaba—a sacred sanctuary that housed various idols representing the gods of different tribes. The cultural and religious diversity laid the backdrop for the emergence of a transformative spiritual movement.

Muhammad's Early Life: Birth and Upbringing

Born in Mecca around 570 CE, Muhammad experienced the loss of his father before birth and his mother at a young age. Raised by his grandfather and later by his uncle, Abu Talib, Muhammad gained a reputation as trustworthy and honest, earning him the title Al-Amin (the Trustworthy).

The Cave of Hira: The Revelation Begins

Around the age of 40, Muhammad began to retreat to the Cave of Hira, seeking solitude and contemplation. It was during one such retreat in 610 CE, during the month of Ramadan, that Muhammad received the first revelation from the angel Gabriel. These revelations, later compiled into the Quran, marked the beginning of Muhammad's prophethood.

The Early Revelations: The Quran Takes Shape

Over a span of 23 years, Muhammad received a series of revelations, gradually forming the Quran—the holy scripture of Islam. These revelations covered various aspects of faith, morality, guidance for personal conduct, and laws for societal organization. The Quran became the cornerstone of Islamic theology and practice.

The Call to Monotheism: Muhammad's Message

Muhammad's central message echoed the monotheistic faith of Abraham, rejecting the polytheism of Mecca. The oneness of God (Allah in Arabic), accountability in the afterlife, and the importance of compassion, justice, and charity became fundamental tenets of Islam. The message faced resistance from the tribal leaders and the guardians of Mecca's idols.

Migration to Medina: The Hijra

Facing increasing opposition and persecution in Mecca, Muhammad, and his followers embarked on the Hijra (migration) to the city of Yathrib, later known as Medina, in 622 CE. The Hijra marks the beginning of the Islamic calendar and signifies a crucial turning point in the establishment of the Muslim community (ummah).

The Constitution of Medina: A Blueprint for Coexistence

In Medina, Muhammad played a pivotal role in establishing a pluralistic society that included Muslims, Jews, and other communities. The Constitution of Medina, a charter drafted by Muhammad, outlined principles for peaceful coexistence, arbitration of disputes, and shared responsibilities among the diverse inhabitants of the city.

The Battle of Badr: Triumph Against Odds

The escalating tensions between the Muslims and the Meccan Quraysh tribe led to the Battle of Badr in 624 CE. Despite being outnumbered, the Muslims achieved a decisive victory, which was seen as a divine validation of Muhammad's mission and strengthened the position of the Muslim community.

The Treaty of Hudaybiyyah: A Pivotal Accord

In 628 CE, Muhammad and his followers sought to perform the pilgrimage to Mecca but faced resistance. Negotiations led to the Treaty of Hudaybiyyah, a ten-year truce that allowed for peaceful interactions between the Muslims and Meccans. The treaty laid the groundwork for a subsequent peaceful entry into Mecca.

The Conquest of Mecca: Triumph and Forgiveness

In 630 CE, Muhammad, accompanied by a large Muslim force, entered Mecca peacefully. The city surrendered without bloodshed, and the idols within the Kaaba were removed. Muhammad's act of forgiveness and reconciliation endeared him to the people of Mecca, and the city embraced Islam.

The Farewell Pilgrimage: Culmination of a Mission

In 632 CE, Muhammad performed his Farewell Pilgrimage, a pilgrimage to Mecca that included a sermon addressing various aspects of faith and communal life. During this pilgrimage, Muhammad received the final revelation, completing the Quranic message. It marked the apex of his prophetic mission.

The Death of Muhammad: Legacy and Succession

Muhammad passed away on June 8, 632 CE, at the age of 63, in Medina. His death marked a critical moment for the Muslim community, leading to the appointment of Abu Bakr as the first caliph (successor) in what became the

Rashidun Caliphate. Muhammad's legacy endured through the Quran, the Hadith (sayings and actions attributed to him), and the establishment of the principles of Islam.

The Compilation of the Quran: A Preserved Revelation

After Muhammad's death, the revelations received during his prophethood were compiled into the Quran. The meticulous preservation of the Quran in both written and oral forms became a testament to its divine authenticity, serving as the unaltered source of guidance for Muslims.

The Spread of Islam: From Arabia to the World

Following Muhammad's death, Islam spread rapidly across the Arabian Peninsula and beyond. The military campaigns and peaceful propagation of Islamic teachings led to the establishment of a vast Islamic empire. The message of monotheism, social justice, and ethical conduct resonated with diverse populations, contributing to the global dissemination of Islam.

The Sunni-Shi'a Split: Early Schisms

The question of leadership and succession after Muhammad's death led to a significant schism within the Muslim community. The Sunni branch supported the election of caliphs based on consensus, while the Shi'a branch advocated for leadership within the Prophet's family, particularly through Ali, Muhammad's cousin and son-in-law.

Muhammad's Enduring Impact

Muhammad's life and teachings laid the foundation for Islam, shaping the beliefs and practices of over a billion Muslims worldwide. His legacy extends beyond religious boundaries, influencing diverse fields such as philosophy, literature, science, and governance. Muhammad's life exemplifies a transformative journey—from a humble beginning in Mecca to the establishment of a profound and enduring legacy that continues to shape the lives of millions.

Chapter 18: Halting the Muslim Advance into Western Europe

In the early 8th century, the collision of two mighty forces, the Franks under Charles Martel and the Umayyad Caliphate led by Abdul Rahman Al Ghafiqi, unfolded on the fields near Tours and Poitiers. This chapter delves into the pivotal Battle of Tours-Poitiers in 732 CE, a clash that would prove instrumental in shaping the course of history by halting the Muslim advance into Western Europe.

The Context of Muslim Expansion

During the 7th and 8th centuries, the Umayyad Caliphate, originating from the Arabian Peninsula, embarked on a series of conquests that extended Muslim rule across vast territories. By the early 8th century, the Umayyads had reached the Iberian Peninsula, establishing Al-Andalus, and aimed to expand further into Europe.

Charles Martel: The Hammer of the Franks

At the helm of the Frankish realm stood Charles Martel, a military strategist and statesman often referred to as "The Hammer." Rising to prominence through his leadership in the Frankish kingdom, Charles Martel's reputation rested on his military prowess and strategic vision, traits that would prove crucial in the impending conflict.

Abdul Rahman Al Ghafiqi: The Umayyad Commander

On the opposing side stood Abdul Rahman Al Ghafiqi, a Umayyad governor tasked with expanding Muslim rule in Europe. Recognized for his military acumen, Abdul Rahman led a formidable force that sought to continue the Umayyad advance into Western Europe.

The March Northward: Umayyad Advance into Gaul

The Umayyad forces, under Abdul Rahman Al Ghafiqi, advanced northward through the Iberian Peninsula and into Gaul (modern-day France). The conquests, marked by the capture of cities such as Bordeaux and Poitiers, raised concerns among the Frankish leaders about the potential threat to their realm.

The Battle of Tours-Poitiers: Clash of Titans

In October 732 CE, the decisive encounter occurred on the plains between Tours and Poitiers. The Frankish forces, led by Charles Martel, confronted the Umayyad army commanded by Abdul Rahman Al Ghafiqi. The clash marked a turning point in the Umayyad expansion into Western Europe.

The Tactics of Charles Martel: A Shield Wall and Cavalry Charge

Charles Martel employed a tactical formation known as the "shield wall," a defensive strategy where Frankish infantry formed a solid line, presenting an imposing barrier to the Umayyad cavalry. The Franks also utilized a disciplined cavalry charge, exploiting weaknesses in the Umayyad forces.

The Intensity of Battle: A Day of Fierce Fighting

The Battle of Tours-Poitiers unfolded in intense combat, with both sides displaying valor and determination. The disciplined Frankish shield wall withstood repeated Umayyad assaults, while the Frankish cavalry executed strategic charges to disrupt Umayyad formations.

Abdul Rahman Al Ghafiqi's Death: Turning Point in the Battle

In a crucial moment of the battle, Abdul Rahman Al Ghafiqi fell in combat. His death led to a loss of command and morale among the Umayyad forces, creating a strategic advantage for the Franks. The Umayyad army, now lacking unified leadership, began to disintegrate.

Frankish Victory: Halting the Umayyad Advance

The Battle of Tours-Poitiers concluded with a resounding victory for the Franks. Charles Martel's strategic acumen and the disciplined tactics of the Frankish forces effectively halted the Umayyad advance into Western Europe. The outcome had profound implications for the future of the region and the balance of power between Christian and Muslim forces.

Aftermath: Implications and Legacy

The Battle of Tours-Poitiers is often heralded as a pivotal moment in history, as it marked the containment of Muslim expansion into Western Europe. While the Umayyad Caliphate retained control over Al-Andalus, the Frankish victory contributed to shaping the cultural, religious, and political landscape of medieval Europe.

The Debate over Historical Significance

Historical assessments of the Battle of Tours-Poitiers have sparked debates among scholars. Some emphasize its importance as a decisive turning point, while others argue that the battle's immediate impact may have been overstated, with broader historical forces at play in shaping the relations between Christian and Muslim civilizations.

Legacy of Charles Martel: Impact on Western Europe

Charles Martel's legacy endured beyond the Battle of Tours-Poitiers. His decisive leadership and military successes contributed to the consolidation of the Frankish realm and the establishment of the Carolingian Dynasty. Charles Martel's grandson, Charlemagne, would further expand the Frankish Empire and become a central figure in European history.

A Defining Moment in History

The Battle of Tours-Poitiers remains an emblematic clash that resonates through the annals of history. While its immediate consequences are debated, the significance of the battle in shaping the geopolitical landscape of Western Europe is undeniable. The confrontation between the Franks and the Umayyads at Tours-Poitiers stands as a testament to the complexity and interplay of historical forces that determined the course of civilizations.

Chapter 19: Charlemagne the First Holy Roman Emperor

In the year 800 CE, in the grandeur of St. Peter's Basilica in Rome, a momentous event unfolded that would shape the course of medieval European history—the crowning of Charlemagne as the first Holy Roman Emperor by Pope Leo III. This chapter explores the significance of this coronation, the political context leading up to it, and the lasting impact it had on the development of the Holy Roman Empire.

Charlemagne: The Carolingian King

At the outset of the 9th century, Charlemagne, also known as Charles the Great, reigned as the King of the Franks and the Lombards. His leadership marked a period of Carolingian rule characterized by military conquests, cultural revival, and efforts to unify the disparate realms under his dominion.

The Lombard Campaign: Expansion into Italy

Charlemagne's military campaigns extended beyond the Frankish territories, reaching into Italy. In 774 CE, he defeated the Lombard king, Desiderius, and assumed control over the Lombard Kingdom, adding Italy to the vast Carolingian domain.

The Papal Dilemma: Alliance and Discord

The relationship between the Papacy and the Carolingians had been complex. Seeking protection against external threats, particularly from the Lombards and the Byzantine Empire, Pope Adrian I had forged an alliance with Charlemagne's father, Pepin the Short. However, tensions arose between Pope Leo III and the Roman nobility, leading to a volatile situation in the city.

The Coronation of Charlemagne: Christmas Day, 800 CE

On Christmas Day of the year 800 CE, during the celebration of Mass at St. Peter's Basilica in Rome, Pope

Leo III surprised the congregation and the Frankish king by placing a golden crown on Charlemagne's head. This impromptu act symbolized the revival of the Western Roman Empire and marked the establishment of Charlemagne as its ruler.

The Title of Holy Roman Emperor: Symbolic Restoration

The title bestowed upon Charlemagne, "Emperor of the Romans," echoed the legacy of the ancient Roman Empire, suggesting a continuity and restoration of imperial authority in the West. This act by the Pope implied a spiritual endorsement of Charlemagne's rule and signaled the emergence of a new political entity—the Holy Roman Empire.

Charlemagne's Reaction: Humility or Ambition?

Historical accounts differ on Charlemagne's reaction to his unexpected coronation. Some sources suggest that he was surprised and even displeased by the act, emphasizing his humility. Others argue that Charlemagne may have been aware of the Pope's intentions and that the coronation aligned with his aspirations for a unified Christian empire in the West.

Political Implications: Holy Roman Empire

The coronation of Charlemagne had profound political implications. It solidified the alliance between the Papacy and the Carolingian rulers, creating a mutual dependence that would shape the political landscape of medieval Europe. The establishment of the Holy Roman Empire laid the foundation for a unique blend of secular and religious authority.

Cultural Revival: The Carolingian Renaissance

Charlemagne's reign witnessed a cultural revival often referred to as the Carolingian Renaissance. Encouraging the preservation and copying of classical texts, Charlemagne sought to revive learning and scholarship within his realm. The establishment of monastic schools and scriptoria contributed to the preservation of knowledge and the promotion of education.

Legacy of the Holy Roman Empire: Medieval Europe

The Holy Roman Empire endured for centuries, playing a central role in the political and religious dynamics of medieval Europe. The imperial title, passed down through generations, became a symbol of authority and legitimacy. However, the complex relationship between the imperial authority and local lords, as well as ongoing conflicts with the Papacy, would continue to shape the empire's trajectory.

The Investiture Controversy: Tensions Between Church and State

In later centuries, tensions between the Holy Roman Emperors and the Papacy erupted in the Investiture Controversy, a series of conflicts over the appointment of church officials. The struggle for authority between secular and ecclesiastical powers underscored the enduring impact of Charlemagne's coronation on the dynamics of medieval Europe.

A Pivotal Moment in European History

The coronation of Charlemagne as the first Holy Roman Emperor marked a pivotal moment in European history, symbolizing the fusion of temporal and spiritual authority.

The establishment of the Holy Roman Empire and Charlemagne's cultural initiatives contributed to shaping the medieval world. The legacy of this coronation resonated through centuries, leaving an indelible mark on

the evolving political, religious, and cultural landscape of
Europe.

Chapter 20: The Invention of Gunpowder

The advent of gunpowder stands as one of the transformative moments in human history, altering the dynamics of warfare, shaping military strategies, and ultimately changing the course of civilizations. This chapter explores the invention of gunpowder and its revolutionary use in weaponry, examining the profound impact it had on the evolution of warfare and the course of human conflict.

The Origins of Gunpowder: Alchemical Pursuits

Gunpowder, also known as black powder, traces its origins to ancient China, where alchemists in the 9th century sought an elixir for immortality. In their experimentation with various substances, they accidentally discovered the explosive properties of a mixture consisting of saltpeter, charcoal, and sulfur.

The Chinese Discovery: Early Applications

While the exact timeline is debated, by the 10th century, the Chinese had harnessed the power of gunpowder for practical applications. Initially, it found use in medicinal and mystical contexts, but its potential as a propellant in weaponry soon became evident.

Gunpowder's Journey Along the Silk Road

The knowledge of gunpowder gradually spread westward along the Silk Road, reaching the Islamic world by the 13th century. The alchemical knowledge and innovations of Chinese inventors merged with the expertise of Islamic scholars, leading to further developments in gunpowder-based technologies.

The Emergence of Gunpowder in Europe

By the 14th century, gunpowder had reached Europe, likely through trade routes or interactions with the Islamic world. European alchemists and military engineers recognized the explosive potential of gunpowder and began to experiment with its applications in weaponry.

Gunpowder Formulas: Composition and Variations

Gunpowder's basic composition—saltpeter (potassium nitrate), charcoal, and sulfur—remained consistent, but variations in proportions and refining techniques allowed for the development of gunpowder with different properties. Innovations in gunpowder formulas contributed to the evolution of more efficient and powerful weaponry.

The Evolution of Firearms: From Cannons to Muskets

The first significant military application of gunpowder in Europe was in the form of cannons. These early artillery pieces revolutionized siege warfare, enabling attackers to breach fortifications with unprecedented force. Over time, advancements in firearm technology led to the development of handheld weapons like muskets and rifles.

The Impact on Battlefield Tactics: Firearms and Infantry

The introduction of firearms had profound implications for battlefield tactics. The traditional dominance of heavily armored cavalry was challenged as firearms provided infantry with the ability to pierce armor and engage at a distance. The shift in military dynamics favored disciplined infantry formations armed with firearms.

Naval Warfare: Gunpowder Transforms the Seas

Gunpowder's impact extended to naval warfare, transforming the dynamics of sea battles. Cannons mounted on ships became instrumental in naval engagements, offering a decisive advantage in broadside attacks and altering the strategies employed by naval forces.

The Spread of Gunpowder Technology: Global Consequences

As European powers embarked on maritime exploration and colonization, they carried gunpowder technology to various parts of the world. The introduction of firearms to different cultures had profound consequences, shaping the balance of power and influencing the course of historical conflicts.

Gunpowder Empires: The Military Rise of Ottoman, Safavid, and Mughal Empires

In the Islamic world, gunpowder played a pivotal role in the rise of the Ottoman, Safavid, and Mughal Empires. The Ottomans, in particular, were renowned for their effective use of firearms, including the innovative Janissary infantry armed with muskets.

Challenges to Traditional Fortifications: The Decline of Castles

The advent of gunpowder weaponry posed a direct challenge to traditional fortifications such as castles. The ability of cannons to breach thick walls and the effectiveness of firearms in siege warfare contributed to the decline of castles as impregnable strongholds.

The Industrial Revolution: Further Innovations in Firearms

The Industrial Revolution marked a new phase in the development of firearms. Advances in manufacturing processes allowed for mass production of more standardized and reliable weapons. Rifling, the spiral grooving inside gun barrels, enhanced accuracy, and range.

The Legacy of Gunpowder: Warfare in the Modern Era

The legacy of gunpowder endures in the modern era, with firearms continuing to be a dominant force on the battlefield. From muskets to rifles, machine guns, and artillery, gunpowder-based weaponry has shaped the evolution of military technology, influencing tactics, strategy, and the nature of warfare.

Ethical and Societal Implications: The Impact Beyond Warfare

The invention and widespread use of gunpowder also brought about ethical and societal considerations. The democratization of firepower raised questions about the nature of conflict, the balance of power, and the implications of arming not just professional soldiers but also civilian populations.

Gunpowder's Explosive Legacy

The invention of gunpowder stands as a testament to human ingenuity, transforming the nature of warfare and leaving an indelible mark on the course of history. From the ancient alchemical pursuits in China to the modern battlefields of the 21st century, gunpowder's explosive legacy has shaped the dynamics of conflict and continues to influence the world in profound ways.

Chapter 21: Norse Explorers Discover and Colonize New Lands in the North Atlantic

The Norse, seafaring people of Scandinavia, left an indelible mark on history through their explorations and colonization of new lands in the North Atlantic. This chapter delves into the daring voyages of Norse explorers, the discovery of uncharted territories, and the establishment of colonies that would echo through the annals of exploration and settlement.

The Norse Seafaring Tradition

The Norse, including the Vikings, were renowned for their seafaring prowess. Their advanced shipbuilding techniques, navigational skills, and adventurous spirit enabled them to navigate treacherous waters and explore far-flung regions, ultimately expanding their reach across the North Atlantic.

Leif Erikson: The Explorer of Vinland

Leif Erikson, the son of Erik the Red, is credited with leading the Norse expeditions to Vinland, believed to be part of North America. Around the year 1000 CE, Leif Erikson and his crew embarked on a voyage that would bring Norse exploration to the shores of the New World.

The Discovery of Vinland: A Norse Outpost in North America

Vinland, likely encompassing parts of modern-day Canada, was discovered by Leif Erikson and his crew. The sagas describe Vinland as a land with ample resources, including timber, grapes, and plentiful game. The Norse established a settlement, possibly in locations like Newfoundland, marking one of the earliest known European expeditions to North America.

Thorfinn Karlsefni: Expanding Norse Presence in Vinland

Following Leif Erikson's discovery, Thorfinn Karlsefni, an Icelandic explorer, led an expedition to Vinland around 1010 CE. With a larger group of settlers, including women and livestock, Karlsefni sought to establish a more permanent Norse presence in the New World.

The Challenges of Vinland: Encounters with Indigenous Peoples

The Norse settlers in Vinland faced challenges, including interactions with the indigenous peoples, likely ancestors of the Inuit. Encounters were both cooperative and contentious, with trade relations established at times, but conflicts arising as well. These interactions shaped the Norse experience in Vinland.

The Decline of Norse Settlements: Factors and Theories

Despite initial attempts to establish a lasting presence, Norse settlements in Vinland faced challenges that contributed to their decline. The exact reasons, including climate change, conflicts with indigenous populations, or economic factors, remain subjects of historical debate and exploration.

Legacy of Norse Exploration: Impact on European Knowledge

Norse exploration in the North Atlantic had a lasting impact on European knowledge of geography. The sagas and accounts of Norse expeditions contributed valuable information to medieval maps and navigational understanding, influencing subsequent European explorations.

Rediscovery of Norse Sites: Archaeological Evidence

In the 20th and 21st centuries, archaeological excavations in places like L'Anse aux Meadows in Newfoundland provided tangible evidence of Norse presence in Vinland. These discoveries corroborated the sagas and affirmed the Norse exploration of North America.

The Vinland Map Controversy: Debates in Scholarship

The Vinland Map, purportedly a medieval map showing Vinland and believed by some to predate Columbus, sparked controversy in the world of historical scholarship. While some consider it authentic, others argue that it is a modern forgery, underscoring the complexities of interpreting historical artifacts.

Norse Exploration Beyond Vinland: Greenland and Beyond

Norse exploration extended beyond Vinland to other regions, including Greenland. Erik the Red had established the Norse colony of Greenland in the late 10th century, showcasing the Norse ability to adapt and settle in challenging environments.

Norse Exploration and the Tapestry of History

The Norse explorations and colonization in the North Atlantic, with Vinland as a focal point, are woven into the tapestry of human history. These daring voyages not only expanded the known world but also left a cultural and historical imprint that resonates through the ages.

The legacy of Norse exploration serves as a testament to the indomitable spirit of those who dared to venture into the unknown, shaping the course of exploration and discovery for generations to come.

Chapter 22: Norman Conquest of England

The Norman Conquest of England in 1066 stands as a watershed moment in English history, reshaping the course of governance, culture, and society. This chapter delves into the events leading to the Norman Conquest, the Battle of Hastings, and the subsequent Norman rule under William the Conqueror, exploring the profound impact it had on the English landscape.

The Prelude to the Conquest: English and Norman Succession Crisis

The backdrop to the Norman Conquest was a complex web of succession crises. Following the death of Edward the Confessor in 1066, England faced a power vacuum, with multiple claimants vying for the throne. The contenders included Harold Godwinson, the English earl, and William, Duke of Normandy, who asserted a claim based on a purported promise made by Edward.

Harold's Ascension and Challenges: The Godwinson Dilemma

Harold Godwinson, Earl of Wessex, was crowned King of England in January 1066 after the death of Edward the Confessor. However, Harold faced immediate challenges to his rule, notably from Harald Hardrada, the King of Norway, who sought the English throne.

The Norwegian Threat: Battle of Stamford Bridge

In September 1066, Harold Godwinson decisively defeated Harald Hardrada at the Battle of Stamford Bridge, eliminating the Norwegian threat. However, this victory left Harold's forces fatigued and vulnerable, setting the stage for the impending Norman invasion.

William's Preparations: The Norman Fleet and the Crossing

Meanwhile, Duke William of Normandy prepared a formidable invasion force. His fleet assembled at the mouth of the River Dives, and in September 1066, the Normans crossed the English Channel, landing at Pevensey on the southern coast of England.

The Battle of Hastings (October 14, 1066): Harold vs. William

The pivotal Battle of Hastings unfolded on October 14, 1066, near the town of Hastings. Harold Godwinson faced Duke William's Norman forces in a fiercely contested battle. The Normans employed innovative tactics, including the use of archers and infantry, ultimately securing victory.

Harold's Fate: The Death that Altered History

The Battle of Hastings resulted in the death of Harold Godwinson, marking a critical turning point. Accounts differ on the details of Harold's demise, but his death on the battlefield left England vulnerable to Norman occupation.

William's Coronation: Becoming William the Conqueror

Following the victory at Hastings, William advanced to London and was crowned King of England on Christmas Day 1066 at Westminster Abbey. William the Conqueror initiated the Norman dynasty's rule over England, introducing significant changes to governance, land ownership, and culture.

The Harrying of the North: Subjugation and Control

To solidify his control, William engaged in a brutal campaign known as the Harrying of the North. This involved devastating northern regions to quell resistance and establish Norman dominance. The ruthless tactics employed during this campaign left a lasting impact on the affected communities.

The Domesday Book: A Survey of England

One of William's notable administrative achievements was the compilation of the Domesday Book, completed in 1086. This extensive survey documented landownership, resources, and population, providing a comprehensive record that facilitated taxation and governance.

Norman Castles: Symbols of Conquest

The Normans erected castles across England, strategically positioned to exert control and suppress rebellion. These castles, including the iconic Tower of London, served as both military strongholds and symbols of Norman authority.

Changes in Feudal Structure: Norman Influence on English Society

The Norman Conquest brought about significant changes in the feudal structure of England. Norman nobles were granted extensive landholdings, displacing Anglo-Saxon landowners. This restructuring of land ownership had enduring effects on English society.

Linguistic and Cultural Impact: The Emergence of Middle English

The Norman Conquest left an indelible mark on the English language. The infusion of Norman French vocabulary into Old English resulted in the emergence of Middle English, a linguistic blend that reflected the socio-cultural integration of Norman and Anglo-Saxon elements.

The Angevin Empire: Expanding Norman Influence

Following William the Conqueror, his descendants expanded Norman influence beyond England. Henry II, William's great-grandson, established the Angevin Empire, encompassing territories in France as well. This extended the Norman legacy and shaped European geopolitics.

The Norman Legacy and England's Transformative Epoch

The Norman Conquest of England in 1066 marked a transformative epoch, leaving an enduring legacy that shaped the course of English history. The conquest ushered in Norman rule, altering governance, society, and culture in profound ways. The blending of Norman and Anglo-Saxon influences forged a new identity for England, creating a historical tapestry that resonates through the ages.

Chapter 23: The First University Is Established

The establishment of the University of Bologna in the 11th century represents a pivotal moment in the history of higher education. As the first university in the world, Bologna set the precedent for organized and formalized learning that would shape the intellectual landscape for centuries to come. This chapter explores the founding of the University of Bologna, its unique features, and its enduring impact on the evolution of higher education.

Rise of Medieval Education: The Need for Institutions

In the medieval period, there was a growing demand for education, particularly in the fields of law and theology. As ecclesiastical and legal systems became more complex, the need for trained professionals led to the establishment of formal institutions where scholars could pursue advanced studies.

Origins of the University of Bologna: A Gathering of Scholars

The University of Bologna traces its roots to the 11th century when scholars, seeking to exchange knowledge and engage in academic pursuits, began congregating in the Italian city. Initially, these gatherings were informal, evolving into a structured institution over time.

The Corpus Juris Civilis: Influence on Legal Studies

Bologna's prominence in legal studies can be attributed to the city's connection with the Roman legal tradition. The rediscovery and revival of Roman law, particularly through the compilation known as the Corpus Juris Civilis, attracted scholars eager to study and interpret these legal texts.

The Student-Teacher Dynamic: Early Structure of Instruction

At the University of Bologna, instruction was characterized by a unique student-teacher dynamic. Scholars, known as "masters," offered lectures and engaged in discussions with students, fostering an environment of intellectual exchange and collaboration.

This model set the precedent for the academic relationship between professors and students.

Independent Student Guilds: The Rise of Universitas

The organization of students into guilds, known as universitas, played a significant role in the structure of the University of Bologna. These guilds, which represented the collective interests of students, negotiated with masters, organized classes, and contributed to the governance of the university.

The Authenticity of Degrees: Papal Recognition

One of the distinguishing features of the University of Bologna was its commitment to ensuring the authenticity of degrees. The papal recognition granted to the university allowed its graduates to practice law and theology with legitimacy, contributing to the institution's reputation and attracting students from across Europe.

The Spread of the University Model: Academic Migration

The success of the University of Bologna inspired the establishment of similar institutions throughout Europe. Scholars and students, drawn to Bologna's academic prestige, carried its educational model to other cities, contributing to the diffusion of the university concept.

Bologna's Enduring Legacy: The University Today

The University of Bologna's legacy endures to this day. It stands as a symbol of innovation in higher education, with its commitment to academic freedom, rigorous standards, and the pursuit of knowledge shaping the foundations of modern universities. Bologna's influence is reflected in its continued relevance as a center for learning and research.

Evolution of Academic Disciplines: From Law to Medicine and Philosophy

While the University of Bologna initially gained renown for its emphasis on legal studies, it gradually expanded its curriculum to include medicine, philosophy, and other disciplines. This diversification reflected the evolving needs of society and laid the groundwork for the multidisciplinary nature of contemporary universities.

Challenges and Conflicts: Struggles for Autonomy

The University of Bologna faced challenges and conflicts, both internal and external, as it sought to maintain autonomy and uphold academic standards. Struggles with ecclesiastical authorities, disputes between masters and students, and competition with emerging universities were integral aspects of its history.

Bologna's Enduring Contribution to Learning

The founding of the University of Bologna marked a seminal moment in the history of education. Its innovative approach to teaching and learning, commitment to academic rigor, and influence on the development of higher education institutions have left an indelible mark on the intellectual landscape.

As the first university, Bologna's legacy resonates through the centuries, emphasizing the enduring importance of organized and formalized education in the pursuit of knowledge and scholarship.

Chapter 24: The First Crusade

The First Crusade, launched in 1096, stands as a defining chapter in medieval history, marked by religious fervor, geopolitical ambitions, and military endeavors. This chapter explores the origins, motivations, key events, and outcomes of the First Crusade, examining its impact on the Holy Land and the broader medieval world.

The Call to Arms: Pope Urban II's Preaching

The roots of the First Crusade can be traced to Pope Urban II's call to arms at the Council of Clermont in 1095. Urging Christian leaders and knights to take up the cross, Pope Urban II sought to reclaim Jerusalem from Muslim control and secure access to holy sites in the Holy Land.

Motivations of Crusaders: Religious Zeal, Redemption, and Gain

Crusaders were motivated by a complex interplay of religious fervor, the desire for redemption of sins, and the prospect of earthly gains. The promise of spiritual rewards, indulgences, and the idea of liberating Jerusalem from non-Christian rule served as powerful incentives for knights and commoners alike.

The People's Crusade: A Prelude of Enthusiasm

Before the formal armies of knights set out on the First Crusade, a spontaneous movement known as the People's Crusade emerged. Led by figures like Peter the Hermit, this unorganized and ill-equipped mass of peasants and lower-class individuals embarked on a perilous journey to the Holy Land.

Formation of the First Crusader Armies: Nobility Takes the Lead

Following the People's Crusade, more organized and well-equipped armies, composed primarily of European nobility, set out for the Holy Land. Leaders like Godfrey of Bouillon, Raymond IV of Toulouse, and Bohemond of Taranto assumed command of these crusader forces, each harboring individual ambitions.

Siege of Nicaea and the Battle of Dorylaeum: Initial Successes

The First Crusade faced early challenges, including the siege of Nicaea and the Battle of Dorylaeum. Despite initial setbacks, the crusaders managed to secure victories, demonstrating their military prowess and determination to press on towards Jerusalem.

The Siege of Antioch: A Prolonged Struggle

The siege of Antioch proved to be one of the most arduous challenges for the crusaders. Facing hunger, internal dissent, and a formidable enemy, the Latin Christian forces persevered and eventually captured the city in 1098, marking a significant step toward their ultimate goal.

The Role of Bohemond of Taranto: Ambitions and Achievements

Bohemond of Taranto emerged as a prominent and ambitious leader during the First Crusade. His role in the capture of Antioch and subsequent conflicts highlighted both his military prowess and his aspirations for personal gain in the newly conquered territories.

Jerusalem Liberated: The Capture of the Holy City

In 1099, after a series of grueling campaigns, the crusaders achieved their primary objective—the capture of Jerusalem. Led by Godfrey of Bouillon, the Christian forces entered the city, marking a watershed moment in the First Crusade and fulfilling the aspirations that had driven them across continents.

Establishing Crusader States: The Kingdom of Jerusalem

Following the capture of Jerusalem, the crusaders established a series of feudal states in the region, collectively known as the Crusader States. The Kingdom of Jerusalem, with Godfrey of Bouillon as its first ruler, became the centerpiece of Latin Christian control in the Levant.

Legacy of the First Crusade: Impact on the Holy Land

The First Crusade had a profound and lasting impact on the Holy Land. The establishment of crusader states, interactions with Muslim powers, and the cultural exchange that ensued left an indelible mark on the region's history, shaping its geopolitical landscape for centuries.

Internal Challenges: Dissent and Discord among Crusaders

Despite their success, internal challenges plagued the crusader states. Discord among leaders, conflicting interests, and struggles for power within the Latin Christian community presented formidable obstacles to the stability and longevity of the newly established territories.

The Reconquista and the Crusader States: Connections and Contrasts

The First Crusade occurred during a period of broader Christian campaigns known as the Reconquista in the Iberian Peninsula. While both movements aimed to reclaim territories from non-Christian rule, the Crusader States and the Reconquista operated independently, each with its unique dynamics.

Reflections on the First Crusade: Historical Perspectives

Historical assessments of the First Crusade vary, with interpretations ranging from religiously motivated expeditions to geopolitical endeavors. The crusade's complexities, multifaceted motivations, and the interplay of various forces continue to fuel scholarly discussions and debates.

The First Crusade and Its Enduring Legacy

The First Crusade, propelled by religious zeal, geopolitical ambitions, and the quest for personal redemption, marked a turning point in medieval history. Its conquests, challenges, and the establishment of crusader states left a profound and enduring legacy on the Holy Land, shaping the course of subsequent Crusades and influencing the broader medieval world.

Chapter 25: Angkor Wat

In the heart of the Khmer Empire, during the 12th century, King Suryavarman II undertook a monumental project that would leave an indelible mark on the landscape of Southeast Asia. Angkor Wat, a temple complex dedicated to the Hindu god Vishnu, would later undergo a transformative shift, becoming a symbol of the integration of Hinduism and Buddhism in the Khmer Empire. This chapter delves into the visionary reign of King Suryavarman II and the creation of Angkor Wat.

Rise of the Khmer Empire: Setting the Stage

The Khmer Empire, situated in present-day Cambodia, was a powerful and influential state during the medieval period. Renowned for its advanced irrigation systems, architectural marvels, and cultural achievements, the Khmer Empire reached its zenith under the rule of King Suryavarman II.

The Reign of King Suryavarman II: Visionary Leadership

Suryavarman II ascended to the Khmer throne in the early 12th century, inheriting a legacy of cultural and architectural prowess. His reign is often characterized as a period of visionary leadership, marked by ambitious building projects and a commitment to the flourishing of Khmer civilization.

Angkor Wat: A Divine Vision

The construction of Angkor Wat, the centerpiece of Suryavarman II's architectural vision, began around 1113 AD. The temple complex was conceived as a grand tribute to the Hindu god Vishnu, reflecting the king's devotion and the prevailing religious and cultural influences of the time.

Architectural Marvels: The Grandeur of Angkor Wat

Angkor Wat, a sprawling complex covering over 400 acres, is renowned for its intricate architecture and sophisticated design. The central towers, intricate bas-reliefs, and vast courtyards showcase the Khmer Empire's mastery in combining religious symbolism with architectural innovation.

Angkor Wat's Alignment: Celestial Symbolism

One of the distinctive features of Angkor Wat is its celestial alignment. The temple's layout reflects cosmic symbolism, with key structures mirroring the path of the sun and stars. This alignment underscores the significance of Angkor Wat as a sacred space connecting the earthly realm with the divine.

Religious Significance: Dedication to Vishnu

Originally dedicated to the Hindu god Vishnu, Angkor Wat was designed as a sacred space for worship, meditation, and royal ceremonies. The intricate bas-reliefs narrate Hindu epics, with the entire temple complex serving as a testament to the Khmer Empire's commitment to religious expression.

The Shift to Buddhism: A Transformative Century

By the end of the 12th century, the religious landscape of the Khmer Empire underwent a significant transformation. The shift from Hinduism to Buddhism, influenced by a succession of monarchs, including Jayavarman VII, resulted in Angkor Wat becoming a revered Buddhist temple.

Jayavarman VII and the Bayon: Buddhist Influence

Under the reign of Jayavarman VII, Angkor Thom, and the Bayon temple, emerged as key centers of Buddhist worship. The Bayon's iconic smiling faces and the pervasive influence of Theravada Buddhism marked a departure from Angkor Wat's original dedication to Vishnu.

Integration of Hindu-Buddhist Syncretism

The Khmer Empire embraced a syncretic approach, where Hindu and Buddhist elements coexisted harmoniously. This syncretism is evident in the artistic depictions, inscriptions, and the overall cultural milieu of the Khmer civilization, showcasing a rich tapestry of religious and cultural integration.

Decline and Abandonment: Factors Behind Angkor Wat's Fate

The decline of the Khmer Empire, influenced by environmental factors, shifting political dynamics, and external pressures, eventually led to the abandonment of Angkor Wat as a thriving center of religious and cultural activity.

Rediscovery and Preservation: Angkor Wat in the Modern Era

In the 19th century, Angkor Wat captured the imagination of Western explorers and scholars. Its rediscovery, coupled with concerted preservation efforts in the 20th and 21st centuries, has ensured that this architectural masterpiece remains a UNESCO World Heritage Site and a testament to the Khmer Empire's cultural legacy.

Angkor Wat Today: Symbol of Cambodian Identity

Angkor Wat stands today not only as a historical relic but also as a symbol of Cambodian identity and resilience. Its intricate carvings, celestial alignments, and evolving religious significance continue to captivate visitors, scholars, and devotees, offering a glimpse into the rich tapestry of Southeast Asian history and culture.

Angkor Wat's Enduring Legacy

The creation of Angkor Wat by King Suryavarman II represents a pinnacle of architectural and cultural achievement in the Khmer Empire. Its enduring legacy as a testament to religious syncretism, artistic brilliance, and Khmer ingenuity underscores its significance in the annals of world history. From its dedication to Vishnu to its transformation into a Buddhist sanctuary, Angkor Wat remains a living testament to the dynamic interplay of faith, culture, and the human spirit.

Chapter 26: The Kamakura Shogunate

In the twilight of the 12th century, Japan witnessed a seismic shift in its political landscape as Minamoto no Yoritomo, under the title of Shogun, overthrew the Taira clan and established the Kamakura Shogunate. This chapter delves into the historical context, key events, and the enduring legacy of Yoritomo's rise to power, marking the beginning of 675 years of shogunate rule in Japan.

Rise of the Samurai: Feudal Japan in the 12th Century

The 12th-century Japanese society was characterized by a feudal structure, with powerful regional clans vying for dominance. The emergence of the samurai, a class of warriors bound by a code of honor known as bushido, signaled a shift in power dynamics and set the stage for the rise of the shogunate.

Taira Clan's Ascendancy: The Imperial Court and the Genpei War

The Taira clan, having gained prominence within the Imperial Court, became a dominant force in Japanese politics. This led to a power struggle with the Minamoto clan, culminating in the Genpei War (1180-1185), a conflict that would shape the course of Japanese history.

Minamoto no Yoritomo: A Vision for Shogunate Rule

Born into the Minamoto clan, Yoritomo witnessed the tumultuous events of the Genpei War, including the exile and execution of his father. Following the decisive Battle of Dannoura in 1185, Yoritomo emerged as a key figure, envisioning a centralized military government known as the shogunate.

Establishment of the Kamakura Shogunate: Yoritomo's Seat of Power

In 1192, Yoritomo received the title of Shogun from the Imperial Court, formalizing the establishment of the Kamakura Shogunate. The shogunate was headquartered in Kamakura, a strategic location that allowed Yoritomo to consolidate power and maintain control over the samurai class.

Shogunate Governance: Decentralized Rule and Regional Governors

The Kamakura Shogunate adopted a decentralized form of governance, entrusting regional military governors, or shugo, with significant authority. This system aimed to maintain stability and control across the diverse regions of Japan while upholding the shogunate's overarching power.

Samurai Code of Bushido: Ethical Foundations

During the Kamakura period, the samurai class embraced the code of bushido, emphasizing virtues such as loyalty, honor, and self-discipline. This code served as the ethical foundation for samurai conduct and contributed to the distinctive culture of the shogunate era.

Mongol Invasions: Shogunate Defends Japan

The Kamakura Shogunate faced external threats during the Mongol invasions of 1274 and 1281. While the initial invasions were repelled by natural forces, the shogunate's preparation and defensive strategies showcased its resilience in the face of foreign challenges.

Decline of the Kamakura Shogunate: Internal Strife and External Pressures

The latter half of the Kamakura period saw internal strife and external pressures eroding the shogunate's stability. Economic challenges, famines, and the inability to address the growing influence of regional samurai families contributed to the decline of the Kamakura Shogunate.

Ashikaga Takauji and the Shift to the Muromachi Shogunate

In 1336, Ashikaga Takauji, a military commander, turned against the Kamakura Shogunate, leading to its collapse. Takauji established the Ashikaga Shogunate, also known as the Muromachi Shogunate, which would govern Japan for the next several centuries.

Kamakura's Legacy: Shaping Japan's Feudal Period

Despite its relatively short duration, the Kamakura Shogunate left an enduring legacy. Its establishment marked the beginning of a long era of shogunate rule in

Japan, shaping the trajectory of the country's political and social structures for centuries to come.

Samurai and the Arts: Flourishing Culture in Kamakura Japan

The Kamakura period witnessed the flourishing of samurai culture, not only in warfare but also in the arts. This era saw the rise of Zen Buddhism, tea ceremonies, Noh theater, and the development of various martial arts, contributing to the multifaceted identity of the samurai.

Kamakura Shogunate and the Dawn of Shogunate Rule

The Kamakura Shogunate, born from the ashes of the Genpei War, heralded the beginning of a transformative period in Japanese history. Minamoto no Yoritomo's vision for centralized military rule laid the foundation for the subsequent shogunates, leaving an indelible imprint on Japan's feudal era and influencing the evolution of samurai culture and governance for centuries to come.

Chapter 27: Genghis Khan

The 13th century witnessed the extraordinary rise of Genghis Khan, a visionary leader who forged a nomadic confederation into a mighty empire that stretched across Asia and Europe. This chapter explores the life and conquests of Genghis Khan, the establishment of the Mongol Empire, and its expansion under his successors, leaving an indelible mark on world history.

Rise of Genghis Khan: From Temüjin to Universal Ruler

Born as Temüjin in the rugged steppes of Mongolia in the late 12th century, Genghis Khan rose from a turbulent childhood marked by tribal conflicts and personal hardships. Through astute leadership, military prowess, and diplomatic skill, Temüjin unified the Mongol tribes, earning the title of Genghis Khan, the "universal ruler."

Mongol Military Tactics: Swift Cavalry and Strategic Brilliance

Genghis Khan revolutionized warfare with innovative military tactics. The Mongol cavalry, adept at swift maneuvering and archery, became the backbone of his armies. Genghis Khan's strategic brilliance, coupled with an ability to adapt to diverse terrains, gave the Mongols a formidable edge on the battlefield.

Conquest of the Khwarezmian Empire: An Early Triumph

In the early 13th century, Genghis Khan turned his attention to the Khwarezmian Empire, encompassing parts of Central Asia, Iran, and the Caucasus. The swift and overwhelming Mongol conquest of this powerful empire showcased Genghis Khan's military acumen and laid the foundation for further expansion.

Organization of the Mongol Empire: Administrative Innovations

Genghis Khan's genius extended beyond the battlefield to the organization of his vast empire. He implemented administrative reforms, such as the Yassa legal code, a system of census and taxation, and a relay messenger system known as the Yam, ensuring effective governance across the sprawling Mongol domains.

Expansion into China: The Jin and Western Xia Campaigns

Genghis Khan turned his attention eastward, launching campaigns against the Jin Dynasty and the Western Xia, extending Mongol rule into northern China. These conquests marked the beginning of the Mongol presence in one of the world's most populous and culturally rich regions.

The Invasion of the Khwarazmian Empire: Conquest and Retribution

Genghis Khan's campaign against the Khwarezmian Empire, led by Shah Muhammad Khwarazm Shah, unfolded as a pivotal moment in Mongol expansion. The swift capture of cities, including Samarkand and Bukhara, demonstrated the Mongols' ability to overcome formidable adversaries.

Death of Genghis Khan: Legacy and Succession

Genghis Khan passed away in 1227, leaving behind a vast empire and a legacy of unparalleled conquests. The Great Khan's death initiated a period of succession and power struggles among his sons, ultimately leading to the division of the Mongol Empire into four khanates, each ruled by one of his descendants.

The Mongol Invasions of Europe: Batu Khan and the Golden Horde

Under the leadership of Genghis Khan's grandson, Batu Khan, the Mongols penetrated deep into Eastern Europe, forming the Golden Horde. The invasion of Rus' principalities and Hungary left a lasting impact on European history, instilling fear and shaping geopolitical dynamics.

Kublai Khan and the Yuan Dynasty: Mongol Rule in China

Genghis Khan's grandson, Kublai Khan, completed the conquest of China, establishing the Yuan Dynasty in 1271. The Yuan Dynasty ruled over a vast empire, unifying China and extending Mongol influence to new heights.

Mongol Invasions of the Middle East: Hulagu Khan and the Ilkhanate

In the 13th century, Genghis Khan's descendants continued the westward expansion. Hulagu Khan, another grandson, led the Mongol invasions into the Middle East, capturing

Baghdad in 1258 and establishing the Ilkhanate, a Mongol
state in Persia.

The Pax Mongolica: Economic and Cultural Exchange

The Mongol Empire, under the rule of Genghis Khan and
his successors, fostered a period of relative peace known
as the Pax Mongolica. This era facilitated economic and
cultural exchange along the Silk Road, connecting the East
and West in unprecedented ways.

Decline of the Mongol Empire: Internal Strife and Fragmentation

In the decades following Genghis Khan's death, internal
strife, succession disputes, and challenges to Mongol rule
led to the fragmentation of the empire. The khanates,
including the Yuan Dynasty, Golden Horde, Ilkhanate, and
Chagatai Khanate, gradually became independent entities.

Legacy of Genghis Khan: A Global Impact

Genghis Khan's legacy extends far beyond his conquests.
The Mongol Empire facilitated trade, cultural exchange,
and the spread of technology and ideas. While the
Mongols are often associated with military conquest, their

contributions to global history, including the promotion of religious tolerance and administrative innovations, have left an enduring impact.

Genghis Khan and the Tapestry of World History

The life and conquests of Genghis Khan, from unifying the Mongol tribes to establishing a world-spanning empire, represent a chapter of unparalleled significance in world history. The Mongol Empire, under his leadership and that of his descendants, left an indelible mark on the cultural, economic, and political landscape of Eurasia, shaping the course of human civilization for centuries to come.

Chapter 28: King John Signs the Magna Carta

In the early 13th century, the reign of King John of England was marked by political turbulence, financial hardships, and strained relations with the nobility. Faced with mounting discontent, English nobles, led by a group of barons, confronted King John and compelled him to sign the Magna Carta in 1215.

This chapter explores the circumstances leading to the sealing of this historic document, its contents, and its enduring impact on the evolution of constitutional principles in England.

King John's Reign: A Troubled Monarchy

King John, who ascended to the English throne in 1199, faced numerous challenges during his reign. His heavy taxation to fund military campaigns, disputes with the Church, and arbitrary exercise of royal power generated widespread discontent among the nobility and the broader population.

The Barons' Grievances: Taxation and Arbitrary Rule

The financial burden imposed by King John, along with his arbitrary actions and disregard for traditional feudal rights, fueled resentment among the English barons. They perceived the king's actions as a violation of their privileges and sought redress for their grievances.

Background to Rebellion: Conflict with the Church

King John's conflict with Pope Innocent III over the appointment of the Archbishop of Canterbury exacerbated the already tense political climate. The Pope's interdict on England further strained the relationship between the monarchy and the Church, deepening the discontent within the realm.

The Gathering Storm: Barons Unite Against the King

In 1214, a group of disaffected barons, led by figures such as Robert Fitzwalter and Eustace de Vesci, coalesced in opposition to King John. Their grievances coalesced into a unified resistance against the monarch's perceived abuses of power, setting the stage for a confrontation that would alter the course of English history.

Runnymede and the Sealing of the Magna Carta

In June 1215, the barons, having advanced through London, confronted King John at Runnymede, a meadow along the River Thames. It was at this site that the Magna Carta, or "Great Charter," was sealed, outlining a series of demands and restrictions on the king's authority.

Key Provisions of the Magna Carta

The Magna Carta consisted of 63 clauses, addressing a range of issues from taxation and feudal rights to legal procedures. Key provisions included limitations on arbitrary royal taxation, protection against unlawful imprisonment, and the establishment of a council of barons to oversee the king's adherence to the charter.

"To No One Will We Deny or Delay Justice": Legal Principles

One of the enduring principles of the Magna Carta is the guarantee of prompt and fair justice. The charter laid the groundwork for legal concepts such as habeas corpus, ensuring that individuals could not be arbitrarily detained without legal recourse.

Legacy of the Magna Carta: An Enduring Symbol of Liberty

While the Magna Carta was annulled by Pope Innocent III shortly after its sealing, it laid the foundation for the development of constitutional principles in England. Over the centuries, its clauses were reissued and reinterpreted, becoming a symbol of the limitations on monarchical power and a touchstone for the development of constitutional governance.

Magna Carta's Revival: 17th-Century England and Beyond

The principles embedded in the Magna Carta experienced a resurgence during the 17th century. Figures like Sir Edward Coke and political thinkers of the time cited the charter as a basis for challenging absolute monarchy and asserting the rights and liberties of English subjects.

Transatlantic Influence: Magna Carta in American Constitutionalism

The Magna Carta, transported across the Atlantic, influenced the framers of the United States Constitution. Its principles of limited government, protection of individual liberties, and the rule of law resonated in the drafting of foundational documents such as the Bill of Rights.

Magna Carta's Enduring Significance

The Magna Carta, born out of a confrontation between English nobles and King John at Runnymede, stands as a foundational document in the development of constitutional governance. Its enduring legacy is reflected in its recognition as a symbol of liberty, justice, and the rule of law, transcending its medieval origins to shape the course of legal and political thought for centuries to come.

Chapter 29: Marco Polo

In the late 13th century, Europe was introduced to the wonders and mysteries of the Far East through the captivating tales of Marco Polo. A Venetian explorer, Polo embarked on a remarkable journey along the Silk Road and beyond, reaching the court of Kublai Khan in China. This chapter explores Marco Polo's travels, the cultural exchange that ensued, and the impact of his accounts on European perceptions of the Far East.

Marco Polo: The Venetian Explorer

Marco Polo, born in Venice around 1254, came from a family of merchants engaged in trade across the Mediterranean. At the age of 17, he, along with his father Niccolò and uncle Maffeo, embarked on a journey to the Far East, undertaking an adventure that would span more than two decades.

The Silk Road Odyssey: Journey to the Court of Kublai Khan

The Polos traversed the Silk Road, a vast network of trade routes connecting East and West. Their journey took them through Persia, Central Asia, and eventually to the court of Kublai Khan, the Mongol ruler of China. Marco Polo's detailed observations and experiences during this expedition would later be compiled into the celebrated work, "Il Milione" (The Travels of Marco Polo).

Tales of the Exotic East: Cultural Riches and Unfamiliar Customs

Marco Polo's accounts were filled with vivid descriptions of the Far East's exotic landscapes, vibrant cultures, and unfamiliar customs. He narrated encounters with civilizations unknown to Europeans, describing paper currency, coal, and the opulence of the Mongol court in ways that ignited the imagination of readers back in Europe.

Kublai Khan's Court: A Glimpse into Mongol Splendor

Polo's descriptions of Kublai Khan's court provided Europeans with a window into the opulence and grandeur of Mongol rule. He chronicled the splendor of the imperial palace, the innovative use of paper currency, and the vastness of the Khan's dominions, offering Europeans a vision of a world beyond their known boundaries.

The Spice Islands and the Marvels of Southeast Asia

As the Polos continued their journey, they ventured into Southeast Asia, discovering the Spice Islands and their lucrative trade in spices. Marco Polo's accounts heightened European interest in the region's valuable commodities, contributing to the later Age of Exploration.

Return to Europe: Impact and Reception

After more than two decades of exploration, the Polos returned to Venice. Marco Polo's accounts of their adventures soon spread across Europe, creating a sensation and sparking widespread interest in the Far East. His tales not only captivated the public but also influenced cartography, shaping how Europeans perceived the world.

Marco Polo's Credibility: Debates and Controversies

While Marco Polo's stories fascinated many, some contemporaries questioned their veracity. Critics doubted the accuracy of his descriptions, attributing fantastical elements to exaggeration or misunderstanding.

Nevertheless, Polo's accounts left an indelible mark on European perceptions of the East.

Cultural Exchange: Impact on European Thought

Marco Polo's descriptions of the Far East influenced European intellectual and cultural thought. His accounts played a role in challenging preconceived notions, sparking curiosity about distant lands, and fostering a more cosmopolitan worldview.

Exploration and the Age of Discovery: A Catalyst for Voyages

The tales of Marco Polo fueled the spirit of exploration that would characterize the Age of Discovery. His vivid descriptions of the Far East, its riches, and cultural wonders inspired subsequent explorers, including Christopher Columbus and Vasco da Gama, as they embarked on their own journeys of discovery.

Legacy of Marco Polo: Bridging East and West

Marco Polo's legacy extends beyond the accounts of his travels. His writings, whether entirely factual or embellished, served as a bridge between East and West, fostering a cross-cultural exchange that contributed to a more interconnected world.

Marco Polo's Enduring Influence

The tales of Marco Polo, whether recounting the grandeur of Kublai Khan's court or the riches of the Spice Islands, captivated the imaginations of Europeans and laid the groundwork for a more interconnected world.

His narratives not only contributed to European exploration but also initiated a cultural exchange that shaped perceptions of the Far East for generations to come. Marco Polo's legacy endures as a testament to the power of travel narratives to transcend geographic boundaries and inspire curiosity about the diverse cultures that make up our global tapestry.

Chapter 30: The Rise and Fall of the Aztec Civilization

In the heartland of Mesoamerica, the Aztec civilization emerged as a formidable force, building a sophisticated society with advanced agricultural practices, monumental architecture, and intricate religious beliefs.

This chapter delves into the rise of the Aztec civilization, its peak of power, and the eventual downfall at the hands of Spanish conquistadors, shaping the course of Central American history.

The Origins of the Aztec People: A Migration Saga

The roots of the Aztec civilization trace back to a complex migration saga. Legend has it that the Mexica people, a Nahua-speaking group, embarked on a centuries-long journey guided by divine signs, eventually settling in the Valley of Mexico. This migration laid the groundwork for the establishment of the Aztec city of Tenochtitlan.

Tenochtitlan: The Majestic Aztec Capital

Founded in 1325 on an island in the Texcoco Lake, Tenochtitlan evolved into a majestic city marked by intricate canal systems, grand temples, and bustling markets. As the capital of the Aztec Triple Alliance, Tenochtitlan became a hub of political, economic, and cultural activity, flourishing as the epicenter of Mesoamerican civilization.

Aztec Society: Structure and Social Classes

Aztec society was structured hierarchically, with a ruling elite composed of priests, warriors, and nobility. Commoners engaged in agriculture, craftsmanship, and trade, contributing to the economic prosperity of the civilization. Slavery, often as a result of warfare, was also present in Aztec society.

Agriculture and Chinampas: Engineering Marvels

To support their burgeoning population, the Aztecs developed innovative agricultural practices. They created chinampas, artificial islands built on lake beds, for cultivation. This engineering marvel significantly increased agricultural productivity, allowing the Aztecs to sustain a large urban population.

Aztec Religion: Polytheism and Ritual Sacrifice

Central to Aztec culture was a complex polytheistic religion, with deities representing natural forces, fertility, and war. Ritualistic ceremonies, including human sacrifices, were performed to appease the gods and maintain cosmic balance. The Templo Mayor, a colossal pyramid in Tenochtitlan, served as the epicenter of religious activities.

Aztec Military: Warriors and Conquests

The Aztecs were formidable warriors, and their military played a central role in territorial expansion. The Triple Alliance, formed with Texcoco and Tlacopan, enabled the Aztecs to conquer neighboring regions, extracting tribute and expanding their influence throughout Mesoamerica.

Arrival of the Spanish: Hernán Cortés and the Conquest

The early 16th century marked a turning point for the Aztecs with the arrival of Spanish conquistadors led by Hernán Cortés. The technological disparity, combined with alliances with indigenous groups hostile to the Aztecs, contributed to the downfall of the once-mighty civilization.

The Siege of Tenochtitlan: A Pivotal Moment

The Siege of Tenochtitlan (1521) proved to be a pivotal moment in Aztec history. The city faced relentless attacks, leading to its eventual fall to Spanish forces. The destruction of Tenochtitlan marked the end of Aztec sovereignty and the beginning of Spanish colonial rule in Mesoamerica.

Legacy of the Aztec Civilization: Cultural Contributions

While the Aztec civilization fell to Spanish conquest, its cultural legacy endured. The Aztecs made significant contributions in art, architecture, agriculture, and astronomy. Elements of their cultural heritage, including the Nahuatl language, persisted and influenced subsequent Mesoamerican civilizations.

The Lasting Impact of Conquest: Aztec Descendants and Modern Mexico

The conquest of the Aztec civilization had profound and lasting effects on the descendants of the Mexica people and the broader indigenous population of Mexico. Cultural blending, syncretism, and the imprint of Spanish colonialism shaped the identity and heritage of modern Mexico.

The Rise and Echoes of the Aztec Civilization

The rise and fall of the Aztec civilization represent a dynamic chapter in the history of Mesoamerica. From the grandeur of Tenochtitlan to the profound impact of Spanish conquest, the Aztecs' story is one of cultural richness, technological innovation, and ultimately, a clash of civilizations that reverberated through the centuries.

Despite its fall, the legacy of the Aztec civilization endures, shaping the cultural tapestry of modern Mexico and reminding us of the complex interactions that defined the course of history in the Americas.

Chapter 31: The Black Death

In the 14th century, Europe faced one of the most devastating pandemics in human history—the Black Death. Originating in Central Asia, the bubonic plague swept across continents, leaving a trail of death and upheaval. This chapter explores the origins, transmission, and catastrophic impact of the Black Death, which claimed the lives of an estimated one-third of Europe's population.

Origins and Transmission: The Path of the Black Death

The Black Death originated in the steppes of Central Asia, possibly in the region of the Caspian Sea. Carried by fleas infesting rats, the bacterium Yersinia pestis found its way into Europe through trade routes, eventually reaching the bustling cities and communities of the continent.

The Arrival in Europe: Trade and Urban Centers

By the mid-14th century, the Black Death had reached the shores of the Mediterranean, facilitated by trade networks linking Europe to the East. Urban centers, with their dense populations and limited sanitation, became epicenters of the epidemic, providing fertile ground for the rapid spread of the disease.

The Three Forms of the Plague: Bubonic, Pneumonic, and Septicemic

The Black Death manifested in three forms: bubonic, pneumonic, and septicemic. The bubonic form, characterized by swollen and painful lymph nodes (buboes), was the most common. The pneumonic form affected the respiratory system, while the septicemic form attacked the bloodstream, often leading to rapid death.

Symptoms and Mortality: A Swift and Deadly Onslaught

The onset of the Black Death was swift and brutal. Infected individuals experienced high fever, chills, and the painful enlargement of lymph nodes. Mortality rates varied across regions, but in many areas, the plague claimed the lives of 30% to 50% of the population, with some areas experiencing even higher losses.

Social and Economic Impact: Disruption and Decline

The demographic catastrophe wrought by the Black Death had profound social and economic consequences. Labor shortages led to increased wages for workers, empowering the surviving population but challenging the established social order. Agricultural decline, abandoned lands, and disrupted trade further compounded the economic fallout.

Responses to the Plague: Medical, Religious, and Social

In the face of the Black Death, societies grappled with a myriad of responses. Medical remedies ranged from the practical to the bizarre, while religious fervor intensified, with some attributing the plague to divine wrath. Socially, fear and desperation often led to scapegoating, with Jewish communities, in particular, becoming targets of persecution.

The Flagellant Movement: Seeking Divine Repentance

The Black Death spurred religious movements, one notable example being the Flagellants. This movement involved groups of individuals who engaged in public penance, whipping themselves as a form of repentance for humanity's sins. The Flagellants believed their actions would appease a wrathful God and halt the spread of the plague.

End of the Pandemic: Subsiding and Lingering Effects

The Black Death gradually subsided in the mid-14th century, but its lingering effects continued to shape European society for centuries. Recurrent outbreaks, known as "plague resurgences," occurred in subsequent decades, reinforcing the trauma and fear associated with the pandemic.

Cultural and Artistic Responses: Danse Macabre and Memento Mori

The trauma of the Black Death found expression in cultural and artistic forms. The Danse Macabre, a genre of art depicting the universality of death, emerged during this period. Memento Mori, reminders of mortality, became prevalent in art and literature, reflecting the profound impact of the plague on European consciousness.

Aftermath: Rebuilding and Resilience

In the wake of the Black Death, Europe faced the arduous task of rebuilding. Communities, devastated by loss, navigated the challenges of economic recovery and social restructuring. The pandemic's long-term effects lingered, influencing patterns of migration, urban development, and cultural shifts in the centuries that followed.

The Black Death's Enduring Shadow

The Black Death, a cataclysmic event in human history, left an indelible mark on the fabric of European society. As communities grappled with loss, economic upheaval, and social transformation, the memory of the plague endured, shaping the trajectory of medieval and early modern Europe. The legacy of the Black Death, while tragic, serves as a testament to human resilience and the capacity for societies to rebuild in the face of profound adversity.

Chapter 32: The Renaissance

The Renaissance, spanning roughly from the 14th to the 17th century, marked a transformative period in European history. Characterized by a revival of classical knowledge and a fervent spirit of intellectual and cultural inquiry, the Renaissance propelled Europe into an era of unprecedented innovation and achievement. This chapter explores the key aspects of the Renaissance, from its origins to its impact on arts, culture, and intellectual pursuits.

Origins of the Renaissance: Rediscovering Antiquity

The roots of the Renaissance can be traced to the Italian city-states, particularly Florence, where a confluence of factors ignited a renewed interest in classical antiquity. The fall of Constantinople in 1453, the influx of Greek scholars and manuscripts, and the wealth accumulated through trade contributed to the cultural awakening that defined the Renaissance.

Humanism: The Intellectual Heartbeat of the Renaissance

At the core of the Renaissance was Humanism, an intellectual movement that emphasized the study of classical texts, a celebration of human potential, and a rejection of medieval scholasticism. Humanist scholars, such as Petrarch and Erasmus, played a pivotal role in fostering a renewed appreciation for classical literature and philosophy.

Artistic Renaissance: The Triumph of Perspective and Realism

In the realm of visual arts, the Renaissance witnessed a profound shift in techniques and aesthetics. Artists like Leonardo da Vinci, Michelangelo, and Raphael pioneered innovations in perspective, anatomy, and naturalism. The emergence of oil painting techniques and the application of linear perspective transformed artistic expression.

Architectural Marvels: Reviving Classical Design

Architectural innovations during the Renaissance mirrored a return to classical ideals. Inspired by ancient Roman and Greek architecture, builders like Filippo Brunelleschi and Andrea Palladio crafted structures characterized by harmony, proportion, and symmetry. The dome of Florence Cathedral and Palladian villas stand as enduring examples of Renaissance architectural prowess.

Scientific Renaissance: The Age of Exploration and Inquiry

The Renaissance witnessed a surge in scientific inquiry and exploration. Visionaries such as Nicolaus Copernicus, Galileo Galilei, and Johannes Kepler challenged traditional cosmological views, paving the way for the Scientific Revolution. The development of the scientific method and advancements in astronomy and physics marked a departure from medieval dogma.

Printing Revolution: The Spread of Knowledge

The invention of the printing press by Johannes Gutenberg in the mid-15th century played a transformative role in the dissemination of knowledge. Printed books became more accessible, fostering the exchange of ideas and accelerating the spread of Renaissance thought across Europe.

Renaissance Courts: Patrons of Arts and Culture

Powerful patrons, including the Medici family in Florence and the Papal Court in Rome, played a crucial role in fostering the arts during the Renaissance. Their patronage supported artists, writers, and scholars, creating an environment where creative endeavors flourished.

Literature and Humanist Thought: Rediscovering the Classics

Literature during the Renaissance experienced a revival of classical forms and themes. Writers such as Dante Alighieri, Giovanni Boccaccio, and William Shakespeare drew inspiration from ancient literature, infusing their works with humanist ideals, classical mythology, and a celebration of the human experience.

Challenges to Renaissance Ideals: Religious and Political Upheavals

While the Renaissance ushered in a period of remarkable cultural and intellectual growth, it was not without challenges. Religious tensions, exemplified by events like the Reformation, and political conflicts, such as the Italian Wars, tested the ideals of the Renaissance and reshaped the course of European history.

Legacy of the Renaissance: Shaping the Modern World

The Renaissance left an enduring legacy that reverberates through the annals of human history. Its impact on the arts, sciences, philosophy, and political thought laid the groundwork for the Enlightenment and the subsequent shaping of modern Western civilization. The Renaissance, with its emphasis on human potential, curiosity, and innovation, stands as a beacon of cultural renewal and intellectual awakening.

Chapter 33: The Inca People Create an Empire

In the rugged terrain of the Andes Mountains in South America, the Inca civilization flourished, eventually coalescing into one of the largest and most sophisticated empires in pre-Columbian America. This chapter delves into the origins, expansion, and achievements of the Inca people as they created an empire that spanned vast stretches of the Andean region.

Origins of the Inca Civilization: Myth and History

The origins of the Inca civilization are shrouded in both myth and history. According to Inca mythology, the god Viracocha created the first Inca, Manco Capac, and his sister-consort Mama Ocllo, who went on to establish the city of Cusco. Archaeological evidence supports the emergence of the Inca in the central Andes around the 13th century.

Rise of the Inca Empire: Expansion and Conquest

Under the leadership of successive rulers, the Inca Empire expanded through military conquest and strategic alliances. Pachacuti, often credited as the ninth Inca ruler, played a pivotal role in transforming the Inca state from a regional power into a burgeoning empire. His military campaigns, notably against the Chanca and the Colla, marked the beginning of an era of imperial expansion.

Inca Government and Administration: The Quipu and Administrative Efficiency

The Inca Empire was characterized by a highly centralized government and a sophisticated administrative system. The quipu, a system of knotted strings, served as a form of record-keeping, facilitating communication and administration across the vast empire. Provincial governors, appointed by the emperor, maintained local order and collected tribute.

Inca Engineering Marvels: Roads, Terraces, and Machu Picchu

The Inca are renowned for their engineering prowess, particularly in the construction of extensive road networks and agricultural terraces. The Inca Road System facilitated communication and trade across the diverse landscapes of the Andes. The agricultural terraces, such as those found in the Sacred Valley, enabled cultivation in challenging mountainous terrain. Machu Picchu, a stunning citadel perched on a mountain ridge, exemplifies the architectural ingenuity of the Inca.

Inca Economy: Agrarian Foundations and State Control

The Inca economy was primarily agrarian, with a focus on the cultivation of staple crops such as maize, potatoes, and quinoa. The state controlled agricultural production through a system of labor obligations known as mit'a, ensuring the sustenance of the population and the provision of tribute to the imperial center.

Inca Religion and Cosmology: Worship of Inti and Sacred Sites

Religion played a central role in Inca society, with a pantheon of deities and a strong emphasis on ancestor worship. Inti, the sun god, held particular significance, and the Inca ruler was considered the "Son of the Sun." Sacred sites, such as the Temple of the Sun in Cusco, reflected the spiritual importance of celestial forces.

Social Hierarchy: Nobility, Commoners, and Ayllus

Inca society was hierarchical, with a distinct social structure. The nobility, including the emperor and provincial elites, occupied the highest echelons. Commoners engaged in various occupations, contributing to the economic prosperity of the empire. Ayllus, extended kinship groups, formed the basis of social organization and collective labor.

Inca Arts and Culture: Textiles, Pottery, and Oral Traditions

The Inca excelled in the arts, with intricate textile production, finely crafted pottery, and vibrant oral traditions. Textiles, woven with precision and adorned with symbolic motifs, served as status symbols and played a role in religious ceremonies. Pottery, marked by distinctive shapes and designs, reflected the diversity of Inca artistic expression.

Chasqui Runners: Communication Across the Empire

Communication within the expansive Inca Empire was facilitated by chasqui runners, highly trained individuals capable of covering vast distances at remarkable speeds. Using a relay system, chasquis relayed messages across the extensive network of Inca roads, ensuring swift communication between the imperial center and provincial outposts.

Spanish Conquest and the End of the Inca Empire

The arrival of Spanish conquistadors, led by Francisco Pizarro, marked the beginning of the end for the Inca Empire. The capture of the Inca emperor Atahualpa in 1532, followed by the systematic dismantling of Inca institutions and the imposition of Spanish rule, brought about the tragic demise of the once-mighty empire.

Legacy of the Inca Empire: Cultural Heritage and Modern Peru

Despite the abrupt end of the Inca Empire, its cultural legacy endures. The architectural marvels, agricultural innovations, and artistic achievements of the Inca people continue to captivate the world.

The heritage of the Inca Empire lives on in modern-day Peru, where remnants of this remarkable civilization stand as testaments to their enduring impact on the Andean landscape and the collective memory of the region.

Chapter 34: Johannes Gutenberg Invents a Printing Press

In the mid-15th century, Johannes Gutenberg, a German inventor and printer, revolutionized the world of publishing by introducing the printing press with movable metal type and oil-based ink.

This technological innovation transformed the way information was disseminated, making books and papers more accessible and affordable. This chapter explores the life of Johannes Gutenberg and the profound impact of his invention on the dissemination of knowledge in the Western world.

Johannes Gutenberg: The Inventive Mind

Johannes Gutenberg was born around 1400 in Mainz, Germany. Little is known about his early life, but he became a skilled goldsmith and a visionary inventor. Gutenberg's curiosity and ingenuity led him to develop a groundbreaking technology that would shape the course of human history.

Movable Metal Type: The Key Innovation

Gutenberg's most significant innovation was the development of movable metal type. Unlike traditional woodblock printing, which required carving an entire page onto a single wooden block, movable metal type allowed individual characters to be rearranged and reused for different pages. This breakthrough greatly enhanced the efficiency and flexibility of the printing process.

Oil-Based Ink: Enhancing Print Quality

Gutenberg's use of oil-based ink was another crucial element of his printing press. This ink adhered well to metal type, resulting in clearer and more consistent impressions on paper. The combination of movable type and oil-based ink significantly improved the overall quality of printed materials.

The Gutenberg Press: A Mechanical Marvel

Around 1440, Gutenberg completed his invention of the printing press. The press featured a movable metal type system, an oil-based ink application method, and a mechanized press to transfer ink onto paper. This ingenious combination of elements allowed for the mass production of printed materials with unprecedented speed and efficiency.

The Gutenberg Bible: The First Major Printed Book

Gutenberg's printing press gained widespread attention with the publication of the Gutenberg Bible, also known as the 42-line Bible, around 1455. This monumental work was the first major book printed using movable type in the West. The Gutenberg Bible showcased the potential of the printing press in producing large quantities of identical, high-quality texts.

The Printing Revolution: Impact on Knowledge and Literacy

The invention of the printing press triggered a profound revolution in the dissemination of knowledge. Books, which were previously laboriously copied by hand, became more affordable and accessible to a broader audience. The increased availability of printed materials played a crucial role in fostering literacy and expanding intellectual horizons.

Spread of Printing Press Technology: Print Shops Across Europe

The success of Gutenberg's invention sparked a rapid spread of printing press technology across Europe. Print shops emerged in major cities, disseminating a wide range of literature, including religious texts, scientific treatises, and popular works. This democratization of information contributed to the intellectual and cultural flourishing of the Renaissance.

Impact on Education and Scholarship

The printing press had a profound impact on education and scholarship. With the mass production of books, knowledge became more accessible to scholars and students alike. The standardization of printed texts also facilitated more accurate and consistent references in academic and intellectual pursuits.

Challenges and Censorship: The Power of Printed Words

While the printing press opened new avenues for knowledge, it also posed challenges to established authorities. The ability to produce and distribute information more widely raised concerns among religious and political leaders, leading to instances of censorship and control over printed materials.

Legacy of Johannes Gutenberg: The Father of Printing

Johannes Gutenberg's invention of the printing press stands as one of the most transformative moments in the history of communication. His contributions laid the foundation for the information age, shaping the way information is produced, distributed, and consumed. Gutenberg is rightfully celebrated as the father of printing, and his legacy endures in the printed word that continues to shape our world today.

Chapter 35: The Ottoman Turks Take Constantinople

In the spring of 1453, the mighty city of Constantinople, the last bastion of the Eastern Roman (Byzantine) Empire, faced a siege that would change the course of history. The Ottoman Turks, led by Sultan Mehmed II, laid siege to the city, culminating in its fall on May 29, 1453. This chapter explores the events leading to the fall of Constantinople, marking the end of the Byzantine Empire and the dawn of a new era under Ottoman rule.

Rise of the Ottoman Empire: From Osman to Mehmed II

The Ottoman Empire, founded by Osman I in the late 13th century, steadily expanded its influence in Anatolia and the Balkans. Mehmed II, also known as Mehmed the Conqueror, ascended to the Ottoman throne in 1444, inheriting a powerful and ambitious empire determined to conquer Constantinople.

Constantinople: Jewel of the Byzantine Empire

Constantinople, strategically located between Europe and Asia, had been the capital of the Byzantine Empire for over a millennium. Its formidable defensive walls, robust fortifications, and cultural significance made it a symbol of Byzantine resilience. However, by the 15th century, the city was weakened by internal strife, economic challenges, and external pressures.

Mehmed II's Ambitions: The Siege of Constantinople Begins

Mehmed II, driven by a desire to solidify Ottoman dominance and establish a new capital, set his sights on Constantinople. In April 1453, he commenced a formidable siege, employing advanced siege tactics, including massive cannons, against the city's defenses. The Ottoman navy, with the aid of a landward blockade, sought to cut off Constantinople from vital maritime support.

The Byzantine Defense: Desperation and Determination

The Byzantine defense, led by Emperor Constantine XI, faced overwhelming odds. The defenders, vastly outnumbered and outgunned, displayed remarkable resilience. They repaired breaches in the walls, repelled Ottoman assaults, and endured relentless bombardment. Yet, the Byzantines knew the survival of their empire hinged on the city's ability to withstand the siege.

The Ottoman Arsenal: The Mighty Cannons and Naval Innovation

Mehmed II's army brought forth formidable weaponry, including massive cannons capable of breaching Constantinople's ancient walls. The Ottomans innovatively transported smaller ships overland to bypass the city's sea defenses, effectively isolating Constantinople from its traditional maritime support.

The Fall of Constantinople: May 29, 1453

On May 29, 1453, after a relentless 53-day siege, the Ottoman forces breached Constantinople's walls. The city, weakened and exhausted, succumbed to the overwhelming onslaught. Sultan Mehmed II entered the city victorious, marking the end of the Byzantine Empire. Emperor Constantine XI fought valiantly but perished in the defense of his capital.

Consequences of the Fall: Ottoman Expansion and Cultural Shifts

The fall of Constantinople had far-reaching consequences. The Ottoman Empire expanded its territories into Southeast Europe, the Middle East, and North Africa, becoming a major power in the region. The event also triggered a wave of cultural and intellectual migration from the Byzantine world to Western Europe, contributing to the Renaissance.

Legacy of Constantinople: Transition to Istanbul

With its conquest, Mehmed II transformed Constantinople into the Ottoman capital, Istanbul. The city retained its cultural significance, now infused with Islamic influences. The Hagia Sophia, once a grand Christian cathedral, was converted into a mosque, reflecting the shifting religious and cultural landscape.

Historical Impact: The End of an Era

The fall of Constantinople marked the end of the Byzantine Empire and the final chapter of the ancient Roman legacy in the East. It also signaled the ascendancy of the Ottoman Empire as a dominant force in the region, shaping the geopolitical landscape for centuries to come. The event remains a pivotal moment in history, symbolizing the ebb and flow of civilizations and the enduring legacy of conquest and cultural transformation.

Chapter 36: Christopher Columbus

In the late 15th century, a daring Genoese explorer named Christopher Columbus set sail westward across the Atlantic Ocean, seeking a new route to Asia. Instead, on October 12, 1492, he stumbled upon the islands of the West Indies, unknowingly marking the beginning of the European conquest of the Americas. This chapter explores Columbus's historic journey, the impact on the indigenous peoples, and the subsequent waves of European exploration and colonization.

Christopher Columbus: The Visionary Navigator

Christopher Columbus, inspired by a vision of reaching Asia by sailing westward, secured the support of Queen Isabella I of Castile and King Ferdinand II of Aragon for his ambitious expedition. On August 3, 1492, Columbus set sail from Spain with three ships—the Santa Maria, the Pinta, and the Niña.

The Discovery of the West Indies: A Fortuitous Encounter

On October 12, 1492, Columbus, aboard the Santa Maria, made landfall in what is now the Bahamas. This encounter marked the European discovery of the Americas. Subsequently, Columbus explored other islands in the Caribbean, including present-day Cuba and Hispaniola (shared by modern Haiti and the Dominican Republic).

The Columbian Exchange: Impact on Flora, Fauna, and Cultures

Columbus's voyages initiated the Columbian Exchange, a transformative interchange of plants, animals, and cultures between the Old World and the New World. This exchange had profound consequences, introducing crops like potatoes and tomatoes to Europe while bringing wheat, sugar, and livestock to the Americas.

Spanish Conquest and Colonization: Consequences for Indigenous Peoples

Columbus's voyages paved the way for subsequent Spanish expeditions led by explorers like Hernán Cortés and Francisco Pizarro. The conquest and colonization of the

Americas had devastating effects on indigenous populations, including the spread of diseases, forced labor, and cultural upheaval.

The First Thanksgiving: European-Indigenous Interactions in the Americas

As European explorers established colonies, interactions with indigenous peoples varied. In some cases, like the famous "First Thanksgiving" in 1621 between the Pilgrims and the Wampanoag people in Plymouth, there were moments of cooperation and cultural exchange. However, such instances were often overshadowed by conflicts and displacement.

The Treaty of Tordesillas: Dividing the New World

To avoid conflicts between Spain and Portugal over newly discovered lands, Pope Alexander VI issued the Treaty of Tordesillas in 1494. This agreement divided the unexplored world along a meridian, giving Spain control over territories to the west and Portugal to the east. This division greatly influenced subsequent European colonial ventures.

Mapping the Unknown: European Exploration Expands

Following Columbus's voyages, European powers, including Portugal, France, England, and the Netherlands, embarked on their own exploratory missions in the Americas. Explorers like John Cabot, Amerigo Vespucci, and Ferdinand Magellan further mapped and navigated the previously unknown regions.

Impact on Global Trade: Silver, Gold, and Mercantilism

The discovery of vast quantities of precious metals, particularly silver and gold, in the Americas fueled European economic expansion. Mercantilist policies emerged, emphasizing the accumulation of wealth through colonies and controlling trade routes. The influx of American silver played a pivotal role in shaping global economic dynamics.

Legacy of Columbus: Controversies and Reflections

While Christopher Columbus is celebrated for opening a new chapter in exploration, his legacy is controversial. Critics point to the exploitation and suffering inflicted upon indigenous populations, leading to reevaluations of Columbus's historical significance and calls for a more nuanced understanding of the consequences of European expansion.

The New World in a New Era

Christopher Columbus's accidental discovery of the West Indies set in motion a series of events that transformed the world. The European conquest of the Americas brought forth immense changes—cultural, economic, and ecological—that reverberate through history. The clash of civilizations, the Columbian Exchange, and the reshaping of global trade marked the beginning of a new era, forever altering the course of human history.

Chapter 37: Portugal's Trading Empire

In the early 16th century, the search for a direct sea route to the lucrative spice markets of India drove Portuguese explorer Vasco da Gama to embark on a historic voyage. His successful navigation around the Cape of Good Hope in 1497-1498 opened a sea route from Europe to India, marking a monumental achievement in maritime exploration. This chapter explores Vasco da Gama's journey, its impact on trade, and Portugal's establishment of a maritime empire.

Vasco da Gama: The Pathfinder

Vasco da Gama, a skilled navigator and explorer born into a noble Portuguese family, was entrusted with the ambitious task of finding a direct sea route to India. On July 8, 1497, da Gama set sail from Lisbon with four ships—the São Gabriel, São Rafael, Berrio, and a supply ship.

The Cape of Good Hope: Navigating the Southern Tip of Africa

The key challenge faced by European explorers seeking a sea route to India was circumventing the treacherous Cape of Good Hope at the southern tip of Africa. Vasco da Gama successfully navigated these perilous waters, proving that a sea route to the Indian Ocean was indeed feasible.

Arrival in Calicut: Opening Trade Relations with India

In May 1498, Vasco da Gama reached the port of Calicut on the southwestern coast of India. His arrival marked the first direct sea connection between Europe and the thriving spice markets of the Indian subcontinent. Da Gama aimed to establish profitable trade relations and secure access to coveted spices like pepper, cinnamon, and cardamom.

Challenges and Diplomacy: Navigating Political Complexities

Da Gama faced numerous challenges in Calicut, including cultural differences, local politics, and competition with established Arab traders. Despite tensions, he managed to

secure a cargo of spices and establish diplomatic ties,
paving the way for future Portuguese trade in the region.

Return to Portugal: Triumph and Recognition

Vasco da Gama's return to Portugal in September 1499
was met with triumph and recognition. His successful
circumnavigation of the Cape of Good Hope and
establishment of a sea route to India earned him acclaim
and solidified Portugal's position as a maritime power.

The Second Voyage: Consolidating Portuguese Influence

In 1502, Vasco da Gama undertook a second voyage to
India, this time as the appointed Portuguese Viceroy. His
mission was not only to strengthen trade relations but also
to assert Portuguese dominance and combat any opposition
from Arab and local powers.

Portuguese Trading Empire: Forts, Posts, and Sea Dominance

In subsequent years, Portugal established a network of
forts and trading posts along the coasts of Africa, India,
and Southeast Asia. These strategic outposts not only

facilitated trade but also served as bases for naval operations, allowing Portugal to dominate the Indian Ocean and control the lucrative spice trade.

Impact on Global Trade: Shifting Dynamics

Portugal's success in establishing direct sea routes to India had profound implications for global trade. By circumventing traditional overland routes controlled by the Ottoman Empire and Arab traders, Portugal disrupted established trade patterns and positioned itself as a key player in the emerging world economy.

The Legacy of Vasco da Gama: Maritime Exploration and Empire Building

Vasco da Gama's achievements laid the foundation for Portugal's maritime empire and significantly contributed to the Age of Exploration. His successful navigation of the Cape of Good Hope opened new horizons for European expansion, paving the way for further exploration, trade, and colonization in the centuries to come.

A Sea Route to Riches

Vasco da Gama's discovery of a sea route to India represented a paradigm shift in global trade and exploration. Portugal's ability to establish a direct maritime connection to the Indian Ocean had far-reaching consequences, reshaping the dynamics of commerce and marking the beginning of European dominance in maritime exploration and empire building.

Chapter 38: New World Foods

The Age of Exploration in the 15th and 16th centuries not only reshaped geopolitical landscapes but also initiated a transformative exchange of plants, animals, and cultures between the Old World and the New World. Spanish and English explorers returning to Europe brought back a cornucopia of previously unknown foods, enriching diets, agricultural practices, and culinary traditions. This chapter delves into the introduction of tomatoes, potatoes, corn (maize), squash, and cacao to Europe, exploring their impact on global cuisine and agriculture.

The Columbian Exchange: A Culinary Revolution

The Columbian Exchange, resulting from Christopher Columbus's voyages and subsequent explorations, facilitated the transfer of plants, animals, and cultural elements between the Americas and Europe. This exchange had a profound impact on both continents, revolutionizing diets and agriculture.

Tomatoes: From Mesoamerica to Mediterranean Cuisine

Tomatoes, originally cultivated by the indigenous peoples of Mesoamerica, were introduced to Europe by Spanish explorers in the early 16th century. Initially met with suspicion due to their resemblance to poisonous plants, tomatoes gradually became a staple in Mediterranean cuisine, contributing to iconic dishes like pasta and pizza.

Potatoes: The Humble Tubers Reshape European Agriculture

Native to the Andes region of South America, potatoes were brought to Europe by Spanish conquistadors in the late 16th century. Initially met with skepticism, potatoes proved to be a versatile and hardy crop, thriving in a variety of climates. They played a crucial role in alleviating famines and eventually became a dietary staple in many European countries.

Corn (Maize): A Staple Crop Transformed

Corn, or maize, cultivated by indigenous peoples in the Americas for millennia, made its way to Europe through Spanish exploration. In addition to serving as a dietary staple, corn became a key ingredient in various European dishes, influencing the culinary landscape of the continent.

Squash: A Native American Staple Finds Its Place

Squash, with its diverse varieties, was cultivated by Native American communities for centuries. Introduced to Europe by Spanish explorers, squash gradually found its place in European gardens and kitchens. Its versatility in both sweet and savory dishes contributed to its widespread adoption.

Cacao: The Bean of the Gods Becomes a European Delight

Cacao, the source of chocolate, was revered by ancient Mesoamerican civilizations. Spanish explorers, including Hernán Cortés, encountered cacao during their conquests. By the 17th century, cacao had made its way to Spain, where it became a coveted luxury item, eventually leading to the creation of the beloved European treat—chocolate.

The Agricultural Revolution: Diversification and Innovation

The introduction of these New World foods triggered an agricultural revolution in Europe. The cultivation of tomatoes, potatoes, corn, squash, and cacao diversified agricultural practices, improving soil fertility and providing new sources of nutrition for growing populations.

Culinary Fusion: New World Ingredients Transform European Cuisine

The incorporation of New World ingredients into European diets brought about a culinary fusion. The blending of indigenous American and traditional European flavors led to the creation of dishes that are now integral to the culinary heritage of both continents.

Challenges and Adaptations: Cultural Shifts in Food Practices

While the Columbian Exchange significantly enriched European diets, it also presented challenges. Adapting to the introduction of these new foods required changes in agricultural methods, cooking techniques, and culinary perceptions. Some foods faced initial resistance but eventually became integral to regional cuisines.

Legacy: A Global Culinary Tapestry

The legacy of Spanish and English explorers bringing New World foods to Europe is woven into the fabric of global cuisine. Tomatoes, potatoes, corn, squash, and cacao are now foundational elements in diverse culinary traditions, symbolizing the interconnectedness of cultures and the enduring impact of the Columbian Exchange.

Chapter 39: The Slave Trade: Enslaved African People Are Brought to the Americas

The transatlantic slave trade, one of the darkest chapters in human history, saw the forced migration of millions of African men, women, and children to the Americas. Driven by economic greed, racism, and exploitation, this brutal trade had profound and enduring consequences for the African continent and the Americas.

This chapter delves into the grim reality of the slave trade, exploring its origins, the harrowing Middle Passage, the impact on enslaved individuals, and the long-lasting legacies that persist today.

Origins of the Slave Trade: Economic Motivations and Racism

The origins of the transatlantic slave trade can be traced to the economic interests of European colonial powers in the Americas. The demand for labor-intensive crops, such as sugar, tobacco, and cotton, led to a massive need for a cheap and abundant workforce. This demand, coupled with racial prejudices, gave rise to the dehumanizing practice of enslaving Africans.

The Triangle Trade: A Network of Exploitation

The transatlantic slave trade operated within the framework of the Triangle Trade. European ships sailed to Africa loaded with goods, exchanged these for enslaved Africans, transported the captives to the Americas, where they were sold into slavery, and then returned to Europe with the proceeds from the sale of slave-produced goods.

The Middle Passage: The Horrors of the Transatlantic Journey

The Middle Passage was the treacherous sea journey from Africa to the Americas endured by enslaved Africans. Packed like commodities in the holds of slave ships, these individuals faced deplorable conditions—overcrowding, disease, malnutrition, and extreme brutality. Many did not survive the journey, succumbing to disease, starvation, or the harsh treatment inflicted upon them.

The Auction Block: The Dehumanizing Sale of Human Lives

Upon arrival in the Americas, enslaved Africans were subjected to auctions, where they were inspected, prodded, and sold to the highest bidder. Families were torn apart, and individuals were reduced to property, stripped of their names, cultures, and identities. The auction block became a symbol of the dehumanization inherent in the slave trade.

Life in Bondage: Plantations, Mines, and Domestic Service

Enslaved individuals faced a life of unrelenting hardship. Whether toiling on plantations, working in mines, or serving in domestic roles, they endured brutal conditions, harsh discipline, and constant dehumanization. The forced labor of enslaved Africans fueled the economic prosperity of the Americas.

Resistance and Rebellion: Defying the Chains

Enslaved individuals resisted their bondage in various ways. From subtle acts of defiance, such as slowing down work, to organized rebellions and escape attempts, these acts of resistance demonstrated the indomitable spirit of those who refused to accept their subjugation.

Abolition Movements: The Struggle for Freedom

As the transatlantic slave trade continued, abolition movements emerged, driven by both moral and economic considerations. Abolitionists sought to dismantle the institution of slavery, advocating for the rights and humanity of enslaved individuals. The fight for abolition gained momentum in the 18th and 19th centuries.

Legacies of the Slave Trade: Racism, Inequality, and Cultural Impact

The transatlantic slave trade left enduring legacies that continue to shape the world today. The racial prejudices ingrained during this era persist, contributing to systemic racism and inequality. The cultural impact of the African diaspora, however, is also evident in art, music, language, and diverse cultural expressions.

The Abolition of the Transatlantic Slave Trade: A Hard-Fought Victory

Abolitionist efforts culminated in the 19th century, leading to the outlawing of the transatlantic slave trade. The British Parliament's passage of the Slave Trade Act in 1807 and subsequent international efforts marked a pivotal moment in the struggle against the inhumanity of the trade.

Confronting the Legacy

The transatlantic slave trade remains a dark stain on human history. Confronting its legacy requires acknowledging the deep scars it left on both the African continent and the Americas. Understanding the historical context, grappling with its impact, and working towards justice and equality are essential steps in addressing the enduring consequences of this horrific chapter in our shared past.

Chapter 40: The Start of the Protestant Reformation

In the early 16th century, a German monk named Martin Luther sparked a religious revolution that would reshape the landscape of Christianity. On October 31, 1517, Luther, driven by his concerns over the practices of the Catholic Church, sent his 95 Theses to the Archbishop of Mainz.

This act marked the beginning of the Protestant Reformation, a movement that challenged the authority of the Catholic Church and laid the foundation for the emergence of Protestantism. This chapter explores Luther's motivations, the content of the 95 Theses, and the profound impact of the Protestant Reformation.

Martin Luther: A Monk's Quest for Reformation

Martin Luther, an Augustinian monk and theology professor, became increasingly disillusioned with certain practices of the Catholic Church, particularly the sale of indulgences. His pilgrimage to Rome in 1510 intensified his awareness of corruption and abuses within the Church hierarchy.

The Sale of Indulgences: A Catalyst for Protest

The practice of selling indulgences, which promised forgiveness of sins or reduced time in purgatory, had become widespread. Luther vehemently opposed this practice, seeing it as a distortion of Christian doctrine and an exploitation of the faithful. His objections laid the groundwork for his later theological challenges.

The Ninety-Five Theses: Points of Contention

On October 31, 1517, Martin Luther nailed his 95 Theses to the door of the Castle Church in Wittenberg. These theses were propositions for academic debate, challenging the authority of the Pope and the sale of indulgences. Luther sought a theological discussion within the Church, not anticipating the seismic impact his act would have.

Indignation Spreads: The Printing Press and Public Debate

The invention of the printing press facilitated the rapid dissemination of Luther's 95 Theses throughout Europe. Translated into various languages, the Theses sparked widespread debate and garnered public attention. The printed word became a powerful tool in the hands of reformers, and Luther's ideas resonated with many who were dissatisfied with the Church's practices.

The Reaction of the Church: Papal Responses and Excommunication

The Catholic Church, alarmed by Luther's challenge, responded with condemnations and attempts to suppress his ideas. In 1520, Pope Leo X issued a papal bull condemning Luther's teachings, and in 1521, Luther was excommunicated from the Church. These actions, instead of silencing him, fueled the flames of the Protestant movement.

The Diet of Worms: Luther's Stand for Conscience

In 1521, Luther was summoned to the Diet of Worms, a gathering of the Holy Roman Empire's leaders. Here, he was given an opportunity to recant his views. However, Luther stood firm, famously declaring, "Here I stand, I can do no other." This bold act solidified his status as a symbol of religious dissent and paved the way for the spread of Protestantism.

The Spread of Lutheranism: The Birth of a Protestant Movement

Luther's ideas resonated with a significant portion of the population, leading to the rapid spread of Lutheranism. Princes and rulers sympathetic to the cause embraced Protestantism, contributing to the fragmentation of religious unity in Europe. The Lutheran Church emerged as a distinct branch of Christianity.

The Augsburg Confession: Doctrinal Foundations of Lutheranism

In 1530, Protestant leaders presented the Augsburg Confession to the Holy Roman Emperor Charles V. This document outlined the key tenets of Lutheranism and sought religious tolerance for Protestant believers. While the Confession did not lead to immediate acceptance, it laid the groundwork for future negotiations and discussions.

The Radical Reformation: Diverse Paths of Protestantism

The Protestant Reformation gave rise to various reform movements, collectively known as the Radical Reformation. Anabaptists, Zwinglians, and other groups diverged from Luther's teachings, emphasizing different aspects of Christian doctrine. This diversity contributed to the complex tapestry of Protestantism.

The Impact on Education and Literacy: Protestantism and Enlightenment

The Protestant Reformation significantly influenced education and literacy. Emphasizing the importance of reading scripture, Protestant leaders established schools and promoted literacy among the general population. This emphasis on education laid the groundwork for the later Enlightenment period.

Legacy of the Protestant Reformation: Religious Pluralism and Modernity

The Protestant Reformation had a profound and lasting impact on the religious, cultural, and political landscape of Europe. It contributed to the rise of religious pluralism, the decentralization of ecclesiastical authority, and the development of modern ideas about individual rights, conscience, and governance.

A Transformative Chapter in Christian History

Martin Luther's act of sending the 95 Theses to the Archbishop of Mainz set in motion a chain of events that forever changed the course of Christian history. The Protestant Reformation challenged the entrenched authority of the Catholic Church, fostering the emergence of diverse Protestant denominations and influencing the broader societal shifts that characterized the early modern period. Luther's courageous stand for religious conscience left an indelible mark on the trajectory of Western civilization.

Chapter 41: Suleiman the Magnificent

In the 16th century, the Ottoman Empire reached the zenith of its power and influence under the rule of Suleiman the Magnificent. A skilled military strategist, reformer, and patron of the arts, Suleiman presided over a period of remarkable expansion, leaving an indelible mark on the empire's history. This chapter explores Suleiman's reign, his military campaigns, administrative reforms, and the flourishing of Ottoman culture during this golden age.

Suleiman's Early Years: Rise to Power

Suleiman ascended to the Ottoman throne in 1520, succeeding his father Selim I. His upbringing and education had been meticulously supervised, preparing him for the challenges of rulership. Known as "the Lawgiver" (Kanuni) in the Ottoman Empire, Suleiman's reign would become synonymous with a period of great prosperity and cultural brilliance.

Military Campaigns: The Conquests of Suleiman

Suleiman's reign was marked by an ambitious military agenda, expanding the Ottoman Empire to its greatest territorial extent. His campaigns included the capture of Belgrade (1521), the decisive Battle of Mohács against the Kingdom of Hungary (1526), and the siege of Rhodes (1522). These victories laid the groundwork for further Ottoman expansion into Europe and the Mediterranean.

The Siege of Vienna: Ottoman Expansion into Central Europe

In 1529, Suleiman led a major campaign to capture Vienna, a pivotal city in Central Europe. Although the siege ultimately failed, it highlighted the Ottoman Empire's formidable military capabilities and demonstrated the extent of its reach into the heart of Europe.

Administrative Reforms: The Kanuniname and Legal System

Suleiman was not only a military leader but also a reformer keen on strengthening the administrative and legal foundations of the Ottoman state. He promulgated the Kanuniname, a legal code that codified and organized various aspects of Ottoman law. Suleiman's reforms enhanced the efficiency and fairness of the legal system.

The Ottoman Navy: Dominance in the Mediterranean

Suleiman recognized the strategic importance of naval power, particularly in controlling trade routes and securing Ottoman interests in the Mediterranean. Under his rule, the Ottoman navy, commanded by figures like Hayreddin Barbarossa, became a formidable force, asserting dominance in the Mediterranean against rival naval powers.

Architectural Marvels: Suleiman's Contribution to Ottoman Culture

Suleiman was a patron of the arts and a builder of grand architectural projects. The Ottoman Renaissance, known as the "Age of Suleiman," witnessed the construction of iconic structures, including the Süleymaniye Mosque in Istanbul and the Suleymaniye Complex, showcasing the empire's cultural flourishing.

The Ottoman Empire's Golden Age: Economic Prosperity and Trade

Suleiman's reign coincided with a period of economic prosperity for the Ottoman Empire. The empire's strategic location facilitated trade and cultural exchange between the East and West. Istanbul, as the empire's capital, became a vibrant center of commerce, attracting merchants and artisans from various parts of the world.

Cultural Flourishing: Ottoman Literature, Art, and Science

Suleiman's court was a hub of intellectual and artistic activity. Ottoman literature, art, and science experienced a renaissance during this period. The Ottoman miniature painting tradition reached new heights, and literary works, including poetry and historical chronicles, flourished.

Hürrem Sultan: Suleiman's Influential Consort

Suleiman's reign is also notable for his relationship with Hürrem Sultan (Roxelana), a Ukrainian slave who became his wife and a powerful figure at the Ottoman court. Hürrem Sultan played a significant role in the politics of the empire, influencing Suleiman's decisions and contributing to the cultural vibrancy of the Ottoman court.

The Decline of Suleiman's Later Years: Challenges and Succession

Towards the end of his reign, Suleiman faced challenges, including the Ottoman-Habsburg Wars and internal strife. The death of his trusted Grand Vizier Ibrahim Pasha and his beloved wife Hürrem Sultan marked a difficult period for the aging ruler. The succession question also loomed large as his sons vied for the throne.

Suleiman's Legacy: A Monumental Figure in Ottoman History

Suleiman the Magnificent left an enduring legacy that shaped the course of Ottoman history. His military successes, administrative reforms, cultural patronage, and the architectural marvels he commissioned contributed to the Ottoman Empire's status as a global power. Suleiman's reign remains a testament to the empire's golden age and the rich cultural tapestry of the Islamic world during the 16th century.

Chapter 42: Ferdinand Magellan's Expedition

In the early 16th century, the quest for new trade routes and the exploration of uncharted territories spurred ambitious maritime expeditions. Ferdinand Magellan, a Portuguese explorer sailing under the Spanish flag, embarked on a groundbreaking voyage in 1519 with the goal of finding a westward route to the Spice Islands.

Although Magellan himself did not survive the entire journey, his expedition became the first to circumnavigate the globe. This chapter explores the motivations behind Magellan's expedition, the challenges faced during the journey, and the lasting significance of this historic circumnavigation.

Background and Motivations: The Search for a Western Route

Ferdinand Magellan, inspired by the successes of earlier explorers like Columbus, sought to find a westward route to the lucrative Spice Islands. In 1519, he convinced the Spanish Crown to sponsor an expedition to navigate the uncharted waters and establish a westward trade route to the East Indies.

The Armada de Molucca: Preparations and Departure

Magellan's fleet, known as the Armada de Molucca, consisted of five ships: Trinidad, San Antonio, Concepción, Victoria, and Santiago. Departing from Seville in September 1519, the expedition set sail with a crew of about 270 men, including sailors, soldiers, and officers.

The Strait of Magellan: A Treacherous Passage

In 1520, Magellan and his fleet discovered the eponymous Strait of Magellan, a narrow and dangerous passage connecting the Atlantic and Pacific Oceans. Navigating through turbulent waters, the expedition faced numerous challenges, including treacherous currents and hostile encounters with indigenous peoples along the strait.

Pacific Crossing: The First European Voyage Across the Pacific

Upon exiting the Strait of Magellan, the expedition entered the vast expanse of the Pacific Ocean. The journey across the Pacific proved arduous, with the crew facing prolonged periods of scarcity, including a shortage of food and fresh water. Magellan's leadership skills were tested as morale dwindled.

Arrival in the Philippines: Magellan's Encounter and Death

In 1521, the expedition reached the Philippines, where Magellan engaged in diplomatic efforts and formed alliances with local rulers. However, conflict arose, leading to the Battle of Mactan. In the skirmish, Magellan was killed on April 27, 1521, leaving leadership of the expedition to Juan Sebastián Elcano.

Completion of the Circumnavigation: Elcano's Leadership

Despite Magellan's death, the expedition continued under Elcano's command. The remaining ships, Trinidad and Victoria, sailed westward and eventually reached the Spice Islands. After securing precious spices, the expedition continued its journey west, successfully crossing the Indian Ocean and rounding the Cape of Good Hope.

Return to Spain: The Sole Surviving Ship

On September 6, 1522, the Victoria, under Elcano's command, completed the circumnavigation and returned to Spain. The journey, originally undertaken to find a westward route to the Spice Islands, had achieved an unintended yet historic feat—the first documented circumnavigation of the globe.

Legacy of Magellan's Expedition: Pioneering Exploration

Magellan's expedition had a profound impact on the understanding of global geography. While Magellan did not live to witness the completion of the journey, the circumnavigation proved that it was possible to traverse the Earth by sea, challenging existing perceptions of the world's size and shape.

The Aftermath: Spanish Claims and Continued Exploration

The success of Magellan's expedition strengthened Spain's claims to the territories it explored. Subsequent Spanish explorers and conquistadors furthered the empire's expansion in the Americas, the Pacific, and beyond.

Magellan's circumnavigation laid the groundwork for an era of global exploration and exploitation.

Magellan's Enduring Legacy

Ferdinand Magellan's expedition, despite the challenges and the loss of its leader, stands as a testament to human curiosity, daring exploration, and the pursuit of knowledge. The successful circumnavigation opened new horizons for global trade, navigation, and cultural exchange, leaving an enduring legacy in the annals of maritime history.

Chapter 43: The Heliocentric Model

In the early 16th century, Nicolaus Copernicus, a Polish mathematician and astronomer, challenged the prevailing geocentric model of the universe, where Earth was considered the center of celestial motion. In his groundbreaking work, "On the Revolutions of the Celestial Spheres," Copernicus presented a heliocentric model, asserting that the Earth revolves around the Sun.

This paradigm-shifting theory laid the foundation for the scientific revolution and transformed humanity's understanding of the cosmos. This chapter explores Copernicus's life, the geocentric model's limitations, the development of the heliocentric model, and the enduring impact of his revolutionary ideas.

Copernicus's Background and Early Observations

Nicolaus Copernicus, born in 1473 in Royal Prussia, was a polymath with a background in mathematics, astronomy, and canon law. His early observations of the night sky sparked a curiosity about the movements of celestial bodies, leading him to question the traditional geocentric cosmology inherited from ancient thinkers like Ptolemy.

Limitations of the Geocentric Model: Ptolemaic System

The Ptolemaic system, prevalent since ancient times, posited that Earth was stationary at the center of the universe, with celestial bodies moving in complex, nested circles around it. This model struggled to account for certain observed phenomena, such as the retrograde motion of planets, leading astronomers to introduce intricate and cumbersome systems of epicycles to explain these irregularities.

The Heliocentric Revelation: Earth in Motion

In "On the Revolutions of the Celestial Spheres," published posthumously in 1543, Copernicus proposed a radical departure from the geocentric worldview. He introduced the heliocentric model, asserting that Earth and other planets revolve around the Sun, challenging the deeply ingrained notion of Earth's central and motionless position in the cosmos.

Sun-Centered Orbits: The Elegance of Copernican Cosmology

Copernicus's heliocentric model offered a more straightforward explanation for the apparent retrograde motion of planets. By placing the Sun at the center and assigning both Earth and other planets elliptical orbits, Copernicus provided a more elegant and mathematically coherent framework for understanding celestial motions.

The Role of De Revolutionibus: Copernicus's Magnum Opus

"De Revolutionibus Orbium Coelestium" ("On the Revolutions of the Celestial Spheres") was Copernicus's comprehensive treatise outlining his heliocentric model. The work challenged prevailing cosmological beliefs and proposed a revolutionary reconfiguration of the solar system. Copernicus, however, hesitated to publish it during his lifetime due to potential backlash.

Copernican Revolution and Its Reception

The Copernican model faced initial resistance, particularly from the religious and academic establishments that adhered to geocentrism. However, over time, astronomers such as Johannes Kepler and Galileo Galilei would refine and provide empirical evidence for Copernicus's heliocentric theory. The Copernican Revolution laid the groundwork for a more empirical and observational approach to understanding the natural world.

Galileo Galilei and the Telescope: Empirical Support for Copernicanism

Galileo's telescopic observations in the early 17th century provided compelling evidence for the heliocentric model. His discoveries, including the phases of Venus and the moons of Jupiter, challenged the geocentric worldview and lent empirical support to Copernicus's revolutionary ideas.

Theological and Philosophical Implications: Clash with Tradition

The heliocentric model sparked theological and philosophical debates, challenging established religious doctrines and cosmological beliefs. While Copernicus intended his work to offer a more accurate description of celestial mechanics, its implications stirred controversy and triggered a reevaluation of the relationship between science and religion.

Legacy of Copernicus: Catalyst for the Scientific Revolution

Copernicus's heliocentric model laid the foundation for a paradigm shift in scientific thinking. His ideas, though initially met with skepticism, paved the way for subsequent scientific advancements. The heliocentric model not only transformed astronomy but also influenced the broader scientific revolution, emphasizing empirical observation, mathematical precision, and the pursuit of objective truth.

A Revolutionary Vision of the Cosmos

Nicolaus Copernicus's heliocentric model shattered centuries-old cosmological dogma, redefining humanity's place in the cosmos. His work marked the beginning of a scientific revolution that would challenge traditional beliefs, encourage empirical investigation, and ultimately reshape the foundations of scientific inquiry. Copernicus's legacy endures as a symbol of scientific courage and intellectual curiosity that transcended the boundaries of convention, paving the way for a new era of understanding our universe.

Chapter 44: Defeat of the Spanish Armada

In the late 16th century, the rivalry between England and Spain reached a climactic point as tensions escalated into a conflict that would shape the course of European history. Queen Elizabeth I, reigning over England, faced a formidable adversary in the form of the Spanish Armada— a powerful fleet dispatched by King Philip II of Spain with the aim of invading and subjugating England. This chapter delves into the events leading to the confrontation, the naval battle that ensued, and the profound implications of England's victory in repelling the Spanish Armada.

Prelude to Conflict: Religious Strife and Political Tensions

The late 16th century witnessed intense religious and political tensions between Protestant England and Catholic Spain. Elizabeth I's Protestant rule and her support for Protestant rebels in the Spanish-controlled Netherlands angered King Philip II. The execution of Mary, Queen of

Scots, further strained relations and heightened the likelihood of conflict.

The Spanish Armada: Philip II's Grand Fleet

In 1588, Philip II of Spain assembled a vast armada, consisting of around 130 ships, with the goal of invading England. The Spanish Armada was a formidable force, believed by many to be invincible. Its mission was to transport an army of 30,000 troops from Flanders to England, overthrow Elizabeth I, and reimpose Catholicism.

The English Response: Defiance and Preparedness

Aware of the impending threat, Queen Elizabeth I rallied her forces and called upon the patriotism of her people. Sir Francis Drake, Sir John Hawkins, and other seasoned naval commanders were tasked with leading the English fleet. The navy, though smaller than the Spanish Armada, was agile and well-prepared.

The Battle of Gravelines: Naval Confrontation

The Spanish Armada set sail in May 1588, but its journey was fraught with challenges, including storms and skirmishes with the English fleet. The decisive Battle of Gravelines, fought in the English Channel in July 1588, marked a turning point. English ships, employing tactics such as fire ships and nimble maneuvering, inflicted significant damage on the Armada.

The Storms of the North Atlantic: The Armada's Perilous Retreat

Following the Battle of Gravelines, the Armada faced further adversity as it attempted to sail north around Scotland and Ireland. Fierce storms and treacherous seas took a heavy toll on the Spanish fleet. Many ships were damaged or lost, and numerous Spanish sailors succumbed to the harsh conditions.

England's Naval Dominance: The Strategic Advantage

The English navy, adept at navigating the challenging waters of the North Atlantic, maintained a strategic advantage. The combination of effective tactics, experienced commanders, and favorable weather conditions contributed to England's naval dominance during the conflict.

The Defeat of the Spanish Armada: A Symbolic Victory

By September 1588, the remnants of the Spanish Armada limped back to Spain. The defeat marked a symbolic triumph for England and Queen Elizabeth I. The Spanish dream of a Catholic conquest was shattered, and England emerged as a formidable naval power, securing its position on the world stage.

The Impact on European Power Dynamics

The defeat of the Spanish Armada had far-reaching consequences for European power dynamics. England's success bolstered its standing as a Protestant stronghold, while Spain's maritime supremacy waned. The balance of power in Europe shifted, setting the stage for the rise of England as a dominant naval and colonial power in the centuries to come.

Elizabethan England's Golden Age: Cultural and Economic Flourishing

The victory over the Spanish Armada is often associated with Elizabethan England's golden age. The nation experienced a cultural renaissance, with flourishing

literature, theater, and exploration. The defeat of the
Armada contributed to a sense of national pride and unity.

Legacy: The Spanish Armada in Historical Memory

The Spanish Armada's defeat became a defining moment
in English history, celebrated as a testament to the
resilience and resourcefulness of the English people. The
event remains a cornerstone of national identity,
symbolizing England's ability to withstand external threats
and shape its destiny.

A Defining Chapter in Maritime History

The defeat of the Spanish Armada in 1588 was a
watershed moment that resonated far beyond the naval
engagement itself. It not only preserved England's
independence and Protestant identity but also signaled the
emergence of the nation as a naval powerhouse. The
events of that summer altered the course of European
history, leaving an indelible mark on the annals of
maritime warfare and shaping the geopolitical landscape
for generations to come.

Chapter 45: William Shakespeare Writes Hamlet

The late 16th and early 17th centuries witnessed an extraordinary flourishing of literature and drama in England, and at the forefront of this Renaissance stood William Shakespeare. In the midst of his illustrious career, Shakespeare penned one of his most iconic and enduring works—Hamlet.

This chapter explores the cultural and historical context surrounding the creation of Hamlet, delves into the characters and themes within the play, and examines its lasting impact on literature and the arts.

Shakespeare's World: The Elizabethan Era

The Elizabethan era, marked by Queen Elizabeth I's reign (1558-1603), was a time of cultural renaissance in England. The period saw the flourishing of arts, literature, and theater, with playwrights like Christopher Marlowe and William Shakespeare contributing significantly to the cultural landscape.

The Globe Theatre: A Hub of Renaissance Drama

Shakespeare's plays, including Hamlet, were performed at the Globe Theatre, an iconic venue in London. The Globe became a central hub for the vibrant theatrical scene, attracting diverse audiences from different social strata.

The Genesis of Hamlet: Sources and Inspiration

Hamlet is believed to have been written between 1599 and 1601, during a period when Shakespeare was at the height of his creative powers. The play draws inspiration from various sources, including earlier Elizabethan plays, historical accounts, and possibly ancient Danish legends.

A Tragedy Unfolds: The Plot and Characters of Hamlet

Hamlet, Prince of Denmark, grapples with existential questions and moral dilemmas after his father's sudden death and his mother's swift remarriage to his uncle, who assumes the throne. The play explores themes of revenge, madness, and the complexity of human nature.

To Be or Not to Be: Iconic Soliloquies and Memorable Lines

Hamlet is renowned for its profound soliloquies, with the "To be, or not to be" speech standing as one of the most celebrated and introspective moments in the play. Shakespeare's mastery of language and expression is evident in the memorable lines that have resonated through the centuries.

Theatrical Innovations: Shakespeare's Contribution to Drama

In Hamlet, Shakespeare employed innovative dramatic techniques, including the use of soliloquies, introspective monologues, and complex character development. The play showcases Shakespeare's ability to explore the human psyche and emotions with unparalleled depth.

The Ghost of Hamlet's Father: Supernatural Elements

The appearance of the ghost of Hamlet's father adds a supernatural dimension to the play. This spectral presence sets in motion the chain of events leading to Hamlet's quest for justice and revenge against his uncle, Claudius.

Themes of Madness and Deception: Psychological Complexity

Hamlet's feigned madness and the pervasive theme of deception contribute to the psychological complexity of the play. Shakespeare masterfully explores the thin line between reality and illusion, sanity and madness.

Shakespeare's Reflection on Power and Corruption

Hamlet delves into themes of political intrigue, power struggles, and corruption within the monarchy. The play reflects Shakespeare's nuanced understanding of the complexities inherent in the pursuit and exercise of power.

Hamlet's Legacy: Influence on Literature and the Arts

Hamlet has left an indelible mark on literature, theater, and the arts. The play's exploration of universal themes, complex characters, and profound insights into the human condition continues to captivate audiences and inspire adaptations across various mediums.

Adaptations and Interpretations: Hamlet in Different Forms

Over the centuries, Hamlet has been adapted into numerous films, stage productions, and literary works. The enduring appeal of the play lies in its timeless themes and the flexibility of its narrative, allowing for diverse interpretations and reimaginings.

Hamlet's Enduring Majesty

As one of William Shakespeare's crowning achievements, Hamlet stands as a testament to the enduring power of literature to probe the depths of the human soul. Its exploration of existential questions, moral dilemmas, and the complexities of human relationships ensures that Hamlet remains a work of timeless brilliance, inviting successive generations to contemplate its profound insights into the human experience.

Chapter 46: The First Permanent Settlement in the New World

In the early 17th century, as European powers sought to establish footholds in the New World, the English made a significant foray into North America. The establishment of Jamestown, Virginia, in 1607 marked a pivotal moment in American history, representing the first permanent English settlement in what would become the United States.

This chapter explores the motivations behind the Jamestown venture, the challenges faced by the English colonists, and the lasting impact of this settlement on the course of American colonization.

Background: European Exploration and the Race for Colonization

By the early 17th century, European nations were engaged in a race for territorial expansion and economic opportunities in the Americas. The English, inspired by the success of Spanish and French ventures, sought to establish their presence in the New World, driven by ambitions of wealth, trade, and territorial expansion.

The Virginia Company: Charter and Mission

In 1606, King James I granted a charter to the Virginia Company, a joint-stock company formed to fund colonial expeditions. The company's mission was to establish colonies in North America and facilitate economic ventures, including the extraction of valuable resources.

Departure for the New World: The Three Ships

In December 1606, three ships—the Susan Constant, the Godspeed, and the Discovery—set sail from England with approximately 104 settlers bound for the Chesapeake Bay region. These pioneers, led by Captain Christopher Newport, aimed to establish a permanent English settlement.

Jamestown's Location: Challenges and Opportunities

Jamestown was chosen for its defensible position against potential Spanish attacks, navigable waterways for transportation, and the hope of discovering valuable resources such as gold. However, the site posed challenges, including marshy terrain, limited fresh water, and susceptibility to mosquito-borne diseases.

Early Hardships: Starvation and Conflict with Native Peoples

The early years at Jamestown were marred by hardships. The settlers faced starvation due to a lack of agricultural knowledge, harsh winters, and a severe drought. Additionally, strained relations with the local Native American Powhatan Confederacy led to conflicts, exacerbating the colonists' struggles.

John Smith and the "Starving Time"

Captain John Smith emerged as a key figure in Jamestown's survival. His leadership and resourcefulness helped the colony endure a period known as the "Starving Time" (1609-1610), during which disease, famine, and conflicts with the Powhatan took a heavy toll on the settlers.

Tobacco Cultivation and Economic Success

The turning point for Jamestown came with the introduction of tobacco cultivation by colonist John Rolfe. Tobacco quickly became a profitable cash crop, transforming the economic prospects of the colony and attracting more settlers seeking economic opportunities.

Arrival of Women and the Growth of the Colony

In 1619, the arrival of the first English women to Jamestown, along with an influx of new settlers, marked a crucial development in the growth and sustainability of the colony. The increase in population and the cultivation of tobacco contributed to Jamestown's expansion.

Representative Government: The House of Burgesses

In 1619, Jamestown established the House of Burgesses, the first representative assembly in English North America. This legislative body allowed settlers to participate in decision-making, laying the groundwork for the development of representative government in the colonies.

Challenges and Conflicts: Indian Wars and Settler Struggles

Jamestown faced ongoing challenges, including conflicts with Native American populations and periodic attacks. The Anglo-Powhatan Wars (1610–1646) strained relations, highlighting the complex and often tumultuous interactions between English settlers and indigenous peoples.

The Legacy of Jamestown: Foundation of English America

Jamestown's establishment laid the foundation for the English colonization of North America. Despite early hardships, the survival and growth of the settlement paved the way for subsequent colonies, shaping the cultural, economic, and political landscape of the region.

Jamestown's Enduring Impact

The establishment of Jamestown marked a significant chapter in American history, representing the resilience and adaptability of English settlers in the face of formidable challenges.

While the colony faced initial hardships, its survival and eventual success contributed to the broader narrative of European colonization in the New World, setting the stage for the development of the United States of America.

Chapter 47: Galileo Galilei's The Starry Messenger

In the early 17th century, the cosmos underwent a revolutionary transformation with the advent of the telescope, a relatively new invention at the time. Galileo Galilei, an Italian astronomer, harnessed the power of this instrument to observe the heavens in unprecedented detail.

The publication of "The Starry Messenger" in 1610 marked a pivotal moment in the history of astronomy, as Galileo shared a series of groundbreaking discoveries that challenged existing astronomical paradigms and expanded our understanding of the universe. This chapter explores the context of Galileo's work, the construction and use of his telescope, and the celestial revelations detailed in "The Starry Messenger."

The Astronomical Landscape of the Early 17th Century

At the turn of the 17th century, prevailing cosmological beliefs were deeply rooted in the geocentric model, with Earth considered the center of the universe. The Catholic Church's interpretation of Ptolemaic astronomy held sway, and any challenge to this worldview was met with skepticism.

The Telescope: Galileo's Instrument of Revelation

Galileo's use of the telescope marked a revolutionary departure in observational astronomy. Though not the inventor of the telescope, Galileo improved upon existing designs and used it to explore the night sky with unparalleled clarity. His telescope had a magnification power of around 20 times.

Construction of the Telescope

Galileo crafted his telescope using a combination of lenses—a convex objective lens and a concave eyepiece. The telescope allowed him to observe distant celestial objects with greater detail than the naked eye, unveiling a new realm of discoveries.

"The Starry Messenger" and its Impact

Published in March 1610, "The Starry Messenger" outlined Galileo's celestial observations and presented a series of revolutionary discoveries. The work consisted of a series of letters, or "sidereal messages," detailing Galileo's observations of the Moon, the moons of Jupiter, the phases of Venus, and other celestial phenomena.

The Moon: A Dynamic World

Galileo's telescopic observations of the Moon revealed a rugged and uneven surface, contradicting the traditional view of a perfect, smooth celestial sphere. He observed mountains, valleys, and craters, challenging the Aristotelian conception of celestial perfection.

Moons of Jupiter: A Miniature Solar System

Galileo's discovery of four moons orbiting Jupiter—now known as the Galilean moons (Io, Europa, Ganymede, and Callisto)—provided concrete evidence that not all celestial bodies orbited Earth. This finding supported the heliocentric model proposed by Copernicus.

Phases of Venus: Evidence for Heliocentrism

Observing the phases of Venus through his telescope, Galileo noted that Venus exhibited a complete set of phases, similar to the Moon. This observation supported the heliocentric model, providing evidence against the Ptolemaic and geocentric view of the cosmos.

Sunspots: Imperfections in the Solar Realm

Galileo's observations of the Sun revealed the presence of sunspots—temporary dark spots on the solar surface. This discovery challenged the traditional belief in the Sun's perfection and unchanging nature, further eroding the geocentric model.

Celestial Controversy: Galileo's Clash with the Church

Galileo's revolutionary findings stirred controversy within the Catholic Church. His support for the heliocentric model conflicted with Church doctrine, leading to clashes with religious authorities. Galileo's work was eventually condemned, and he faced trial by the Roman Catholic Inquisition in 1633.

Legacy of "The Starry Messenger": A New Vision of the Cosmos

Despite the challenges and censure, "The Starry Messenger" significantly altered humanity's perception of the cosmos. Galileo's empirical approach to astronomy laid the groundwork for modern observational techniques and influenced subsequent scientific revolutions.

Galileo's Celestial Revolution

Galileo Galilei's publication of "The Starry Messenger" was a pivotal moment in the history of astronomy. Through the lens of his telescope, he unveiled a cosmos vastly different from the traditional, Earth-centered view.

Galileo's courage in challenging established dogma and his contributions to observational astronomy paved the way for a scientific renaissance, transforming our understanding of the universe and inspiring generations of astronomers to come.

Chapter 48: England's Civil War

The 17th century witnessed a tumultuous period in English history marked by political, religious, and social upheaval, culminating in a devastating civil war. The English Civil War, also known as the Puritan Revolution, erupted in 1642 and continued for nearly a decade, profoundly reshaping the political landscape of England. This chapter explores the background leading to the conflict, the key players involved, major battles, and the consequences that reverberated through English society.

Background: Seeds of Discontent

In the early 17th century, tensions between the monarchy and Parliament escalated, fueled by disputes over taxation, religious policies, and the scope of royal authority. The Stuart kings, particularly Charles I, faced growing resistance as they sought to assert absolute rule.

Charles I and the Struggle for Royal Authority

Charles I's attempts to levy taxes without parliamentary consent and his adherence to High Anglicanism antagonized Parliament and a significant portion of the population. The king's perceived absolutism clashed with the emerging principles of parliamentary sovereignty.

The Role of Religion: Rise of Puritanism

Religious tensions played a crucial role in the lead-up to the Civil War. The rise of Puritanism and its influence within Parliament created a fervently Protestant faction that resisted the king's attempts to impose religious conformity.

The Petition of Right (1628) and Charles I's Dissolution of Parliament

The Petition of Right, a parliamentary document of 1628, sought to limit the king's powers by prohibiting arbitrary taxation and imprisonment. Charles I, however, dissolved Parliament multiple times, intensifying the conflict and deepening the divide between royalists and parliamentarians.

The Short Parliament and the Long Parliament

In 1640, Charles I recalled Parliament due to financial constraints caused by the Bishops' Wars with Scotland. The resulting "Short Parliament" was quickly dissolved. The subsequent "Long Parliament," convened later in 1640, became a focal point for opposition to the king's policies.

Archbishop Laud's Trial and Execution

The Long Parliament initiated reforms and sought to hold key royal advisors accountable. Archbishop William Laud, a figure associated with Charles I's religious policies, was impeached, tried, and executed in 1645, symbolizing the growing power of Parliament.

The Outbreak of War: Royalists vs. Parliamentarians

Tensions escalated into armed conflict in 1642 when Charles I attempted to arrest five members of Parliament. The country became divided between royalists (Cavaliers), who supported the king, and parliamentarians (Roundheads), who opposed royal absolutism.

Key Battles: Edgehill, Marston Moor, and Naseby

The English Civil War featured several significant battles. The Battle of Edgehill (1642) marked the war's outset, followed by pivotal clashes at Marston Moor (1644) and Naseby (1645). These engagements shifted the balance of power and determined the course of the conflict.

Oliver Cromwell and the New Model Army

Oliver Cromwell emerged as a key figure within the parliamentarian forces. The formation of the New Model Army, a professional military force, under Cromwell's leadership proved decisive in the later stages of the war.

The Execution of Charles I and the Interregnum

The conflict reached a critical juncture with the capture of Charles I by parliamentarian forces. In 1649, following a trial, Charles I was executed, leading to the establishment of the Commonwealth of England under Oliver Cromwell and the interregnum period.

The Restoration: Charles II and the Monarchy's Return

The death of Cromwell in 1658 and the subsequent collapse of the Protectorate paved the way for the restoration of the monarchy. In 1660, Charles II, the son of Charles I, was invited to return from exile, marking the end of the English Republic.

Consequences and Legacy: Constitutional Changes and Political Evolution

The English Civil War had profound consequences, leading to significant constitutional changes. The Glorious Revolution of 1688 further shaped the evolution of parliamentary democracy, emphasizing limits on royal power and the supremacy of Parliament.

The Impact of the English Civil War

The English Civil War stands as a watershed moment in English history, reshaping the balance of power between monarchy and Parliament. The conflict laid the groundwork for constitutional developments, influencing the trajectory of political and social structures for centuries to come. The scars of the Civil War lingered in the national consciousness, influencing discussions on governance, liberty, and the role of the state.

Chapter 49: The Taj Mahal

In the 17th century, during the height of the Mughal Empire, one of the most magnificent architectural wonders in the world emerged—the Taj Mahal. Commissioned by the fifth Mughal Emperor, Shah Jahan, the Taj Mahal stands as an enduring symbol of love and devotion. This chapter explores the historical context of its construction, the architectural marvels of the Taj Mahal, and the poignant love story that inspired its creation.

The Mughal Empire in the 17th Century

At its zenith, the Mughal Empire under Shah Jahan (1628–1658) was a flourishing center of culture, art, and architecture. Known for its grandeur and opulence, the empire reached its peak during the rule of Shah Jahan, who sought to leave an indelible mark on the landscape.

Shah Jahan's Love Story with Mumtaz Mahal

The construction of the Taj Mahal was motivated by the profound love between Shah Jahan and his favorite wife,

Mumtaz Mahal. Mumtaz, whose name means "Chosen One of the Palace," held a special place in the emperor's heart, and her untimely death in 1631 during childbirth deeply affected Shah Jahan.

The Concept of the Taj Mahal: A Symbol of Eternal Love

In grief and admiration for Mumtaz, Shah Jahan conceived the idea of building a mausoleum that would not only serve as her final resting place but also immortalize their love. The Taj Mahal was envisioned as a testament to the emperor's enduring devotion to Mumtaz.

Architectural Marvels of the Taj Mahal

The Taj Mahal, designed by architect Ustad Ahmad Lahori, is a masterpiece of Mughal architecture. The white marble structure incorporates elements of Persian, Indian, and Islamic architecture, showcasing a harmonious blend of form, symmetry, and intricate detailing.

Construction Materials and Techniques

The Taj Mahal is primarily constructed from white marble sourced from Makrana in Rajasthan. The meticulous craftsmanship involves the use of semiprecious stones, such as lapis lazuli and jade, for intricate inlay work known as pietra dura. The central dome, minarets, and detailed geometric patterns contribute to the monument's aesthetic allure.

Layout and Design: Symbolism in Every Detail

The Taj Mahal is set within a charbagh, a Persian-style garden divided into four quadrants by water channels. The mausoleum's symmetrical layout symbolizes the paradisiacal garden of Islam. The central onion-shaped dome, minarets, and intricate calligraphy on the façade add to the architectural splendor.

Construction Timeline: A Labor of Love

Construction of the Taj Mahal began in 1632 and continued for over two decades, involving the efforts of thousands of artisans and laborers. The monument's completion in 1653 marked the culmination of a monumental architectural undertaking that reflected the emperor's enduring commitment to Mumtaz.

Mumtaz Mahal's Final Resting Place

The inner sanctum of the Taj Mahal houses the cenotaphs of Mumtaz Mahal and Shah Jahan, adorned with delicate marble inlay. The actual graves lie in a chamber below the main floor, accessible to visitors.

Shah Jahan's Vision Realized: The Taj Mahal's Legacy

The Taj Mahal is not merely a mausoleum but a symbol of enduring love and artistic brilliance. Shah Jahan's vision of eternalizing his love for Mumtaz through this architectural marvel has ensured the Taj Mahal's enduring legacy as one of the Seven Wonders of the World.

Conservation Efforts and UNESCO World Heritage Status

Recognizing the Taj Mahal's cultural significance, it was designated a UNESCO World Heritage Site in 1983. Conservation efforts have been ongoing to preserve its pristine beauty, addressing challenges such as pollution, weathering, and the impact of tourism.

The Taj Mahal's Timeless Grandeur

The Taj Mahal remains an iconic testament to the power of love, art, and architectural innovation. Its ethereal beauty and poignant history continue to captivate visitors from around the globe, making the Taj Mahal an everlasting symbol of enduring love and a jewel in the crown of Mughal architecture.

Chapter 50: The Steam Engine

The 18th century witnessed a transformative technological revolution with the advent of the steam engine, a groundbreaking invention that would propel the Industrial Revolution.

The harnessing of steam power marked a pivotal moment in history, transforming industries, transportation, and ultimately, the way people lived and worked. This chapter explores the origins, development, and profound impact of the steam engine on society.

The Predecessors: Early Experiments with Steam Power

Before the full emergence of the steam engine, inventors and engineers conducted various experiments involving steam. Notable figures such as Hero of Alexandria and Denis Papin contributed to the understanding of steam's potential as a source of power.

Thomas Newcomen's Atmospheric Engine

In 1712, Thomas Newcomen, an English engineer, developed the first practical steam engine—the atmospheric engine. This engine utilized atmospheric pressure to move a piston within a cylinder, marking a significant step in harnessing steam power for industrial use.

James Watt's Improvements: The Birth of the Watt Steam Engine

James Watt, a Scottish engineer, made crucial improvements to the steam engine in the mid-18th century. Watt introduced a separate condenser, rotary motion, and other enhancements, creating the Watt steam engine. His innovations greatly increased the engine's efficiency and laid the foundation for its widespread adoption.

The Industrial Revolution is Set in Motion

The Watt steam engine played a pivotal role in driving the Industrial Revolution. Its widespread use in various industries, particularly textile manufacturing and mining, revolutionized production processes and led to unprecedented economic and social changes.

Steam Engines in Manufacturing: The Textile Industry

Steam engines were instrumental in powering machinery in textile mills. The mechanization of spinning and weaving processes increased production efficiency, reduced costs, and laid the groundwork for the factory system.

Steam Power and Mining: Extracting Resources on a New Scale

The steam engine transformed the mining industry by enabling the efficient drainage of water from mines. Steam-powered pumps and engines facilitated deeper and more extensive mining operations, ensuring a steady supply of raw materials for industries.

Transportation Revolution: Steam Locomotives and Steamboats

The application of steam power to transportation revolutionized the movement of goods and people. Steam locomotives, pioneered by figures like George Stephenson, provided faster and more reliable land transportation, while steamboats navigated rivers and opened up new avenues for trade and travel.

Steam Engines in Agriculture: Increased Productivity

The use of steam engines in agriculture brought about increased efficiency in tasks such as plowing, threshing, and milling. The adoption of steam-powered machinery transformed traditional farming methods, contributing to the growth of agricultural productivity.

Challenges and Innovations: Overcoming Limitations

While the steam engine offered unprecedented benefits, it also faced challenges, such as the need for a constant water supply and the inefficiency of early designs. Innovations and adaptations addressed these limitations, contributing to the continuous improvement of steam engine technology.

Impact on Society: Social and Economic Transformations

The steam engine's impact reverberated throughout society, fostering urbanization, creating new economic opportunities, and shaping the emergence of a modern industrial society. The factory system, urban centers, and the rise of a working class were all influenced by the transformative power of steam.

Environmental Impact: The Steam Engine and Industrialization

The widespread use of steam power had significant environmental consequences, including deforestation for fuel and the release of pollutants. These environmental challenges prompted later innovations in steam engine design and alternative energy sources.

Legacy: The Enduring Influence of Steam Power

The steam engine's legacy endures in the technological advancements it spurred and the profound changes it brought to society. While subsequent innovations, such as electric power, replaced steam in many applications, the steam engine remains a symbol of the Industrial Revolution and a testament to humanity's ability to harness and control natural forces for progress.

The Steam Engine's Enduring Significance

The harnessing of steam power through the invention and refinement of the steam engine stands as a watershed moment in history. From powering factories to revolutionizing transportation, the steam engine played a central role in shaping the modern world.

Its impact on industry, commerce, and daily life laid the groundwork for subsequent technological revolutions, leaving an enduring legacy that continues to influence the course of human progress.

www.ingramcontent.com/pod-product-compliance
Lightning Source LLC
Chambersburg PA
CBHW070923260726
48661CB00003B/809